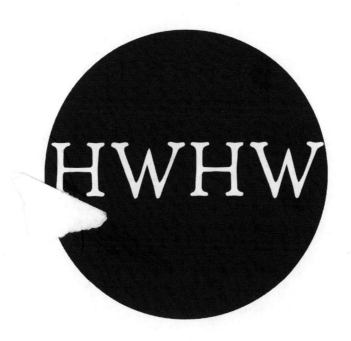

SIGNAL
AND
NOISE

ADVANCED
PSYCHIC TRAINING
for Remote Viewing,
Clairvoyance, and ESP

SEAN MCNAMARA

## About "Signal and Noise"

- Includes training with many exercises
- Filled with exciting photos of targets and transcripts
- Shows exactly how a team used this to win a small lottery twice

Also on Audiobook

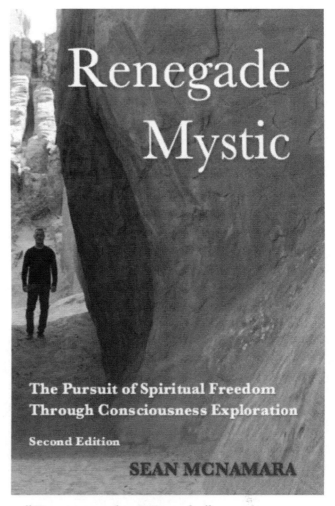

Renegade Mystic

The Pursuit of Spiritual Freedom Through Consciousness Exploration

Second Edition

SEAN MCNAMARA

## About "Renegade Mystic"

- Spiritual Memoir about Self-Empowerment
- Instructions for Out of Body Experiences and Lucid Dreaming
- Avoiding harmful teachers and groups
- Other topics: Clairvoyance, Precognition, Mediumship, UFO & non-human contact
- Perfect for road trips to mysterious places

## About "Defy Your Limits"

- The most thorough training instructions for learning telekinesis (mind over matter)

- Includes links to videos on the book's website

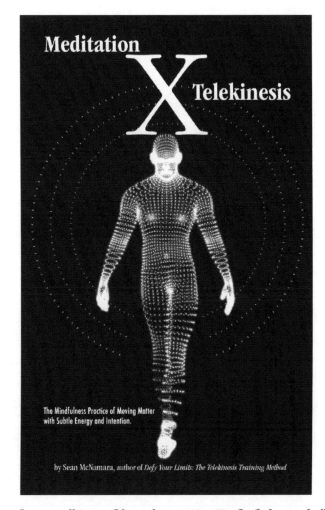

**Meditation X Telekinesis**

The Mindfulness Practice of Moving Matter with Subtle Energy and Intention.

by Sean McNamara, author of *Defy Your Limits: The Telekinesis Training Method*

## About "Meditation X: Telekinesis"

- Telekinesis as a valid form of meditation

- Complex/next-level telekinesis exercises for those who learned the basics in "Defy Your Limits"

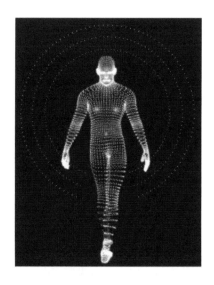

# Mind Sight

## TRAINING TO SEE WITHOUT EYES

### Pilot Program for Adults

SEAN MCNAMARA

First Edition

Published by
Mind Possible

www.MindPossible.com

ISBN: 978-1-7352930-4-2

1. Psychic Development    2. Paranormal and ESP
3. New Age & Supernatural  4. Self-Help

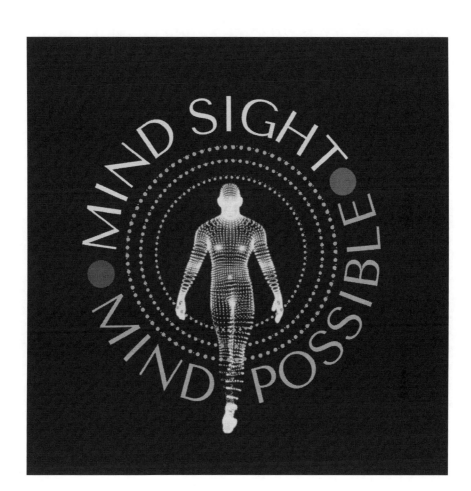

# TABLE OF CONTENTS

Acknowledgment and Dedication ...............................1

## PART 1 - THE FOUNDATION

Introduction ...............................................8
How to Use this Book ...................................... 14
    The 14 Phases ........................................ 15
    Going Rogue ......................................... 16
    Cross Training and Boredom Busters ...............17
    It's All Right to Stop Any Time ..................... 23
    For Teachers ........................................ 24
    What You Say Matters ............................... 24
Concepts and Questions ................................... 26
    Get Your "Thinking" Over with Before Training . 26
    How Does Mind Sight Work? ...................... 27
    The Consciousness Connection ...................... 29
    Can I *Really* Learn to Do This?...................... 33
    Avoid the Decline Effect ............................ 34
To Become Like Children ................................. 35
Preparatory Exercises ..................................... 39
    Dream Recollection .................................. 40
    Spontaneous Daytime Exercises ..................... 42
    Guided Visualizations ............................... 43
    Guided Meditations ................................. 44
    The Color Wheel - Redux ........................... 44
Brain Training ............................................ 46
Attitudes for Success ..................................... 49
Learn from My Mistakes .................................. 50
Notes from the Field ...................................... 53

## PART 2 - ACROSS SPACE AND TIME

Remote Viewers, Meet the Seers. Seers, Meet the
Remote Viewers ..........................................72
Precognition and Retrocognition ..........................76

Long Distance Perception and Telepathy ...................... 83

PART 3 - THE TRAINING

Required Materials ............................................... 88
The Glue Technique .............................................. 90
Working with Color .............................................. 92
Windows of Perception ........................................... 93
Using the Training Journal ...................................... 94

Phase 1- Color Familiarization ................................. 95
Phase 2 - Two Color Perception ................................. 107
Phase 3 - Three Color Perception ...............................119
Phase 4 - Five Color Perception ...............................155
Phase 5 - Contrasting Black and White .........................167
Phase 6 - Shapes (Touching Paper) ............................. 182
Phase 7 - Colored Shapes ...................................... 195
Phase 8 - Numbers ............................................. .206

Using Your Fingertip as a Guide ............................... 209

Phase 9 - Capital Letters ..................................... 237
Phase 10 - Lower Case Letters ................................. 259
Phase 11 - Upper and Lower Case Counterparts ............. 281
Phase 12 - Upper Case Words ................................... 297
Phase 13 - Lower Case Words ................................... 308
Phase 14 - Capitalized Words .................................. 319

Next Steps .................................................... 326
Recommended Reading ........................................... 327
Index ......................................................... 329
About the Author .............................................. 330

# ACKNOWLEDGMENT AND DEDICATION

Let us begin with a story from the ancient days:

One night, on the outskirts of a village, a group of eager pupils sat before a famous teacher of spiritual knowledge. The wise elder gazed upon them and spoke slowly.

He told them, "Now, I will give you the secret mantra. This mantra has the power to reveal hidden secrets, empower people of all ages and from all nations, and grant them a sense of purpose and meaning. I will tell you this mantra now, but you must keep it a secret. Do not tell a single soul! Stay away from the village. Then, return here to me tomorrow night and I will initiate those of you who are worthy to carry on my lineage."

The pupils left the wise elder and went their separate ways for the night, eager to return the following evening to receive their reward for keeping the mantra a secret. But, two of them met on the road leading back to the village.

The man asked, "Why are you going this way?"

The woman replied, "Aren't you walking the same path as I?"

He decided to confide in her, "This world is a difficult place, is it not? So many people are searching for ways to understand themselves and explore what it means to be alive. But many teachers hold their knowledge inside of closed fists."

She nodded in agreement and said, "Yes! And we've been given this mantra which could help people everywhere, but we've been told to keep it a secret. Yet, I can't bear the thought of withholding this when it would be so easy to help so many. I cannot keep the secret!"

He laughed, understanding they were already in agreement. "I can't either! What would be the point of keeping this knowledge to ourselves? I'm willing to tell the whole village the secret mantra tonight if you'll help me. And I don't care if the master punishes us tomorrow night. Are you with me?"

And she was. They entered the village and began to share the mantra with anyone who would listen, trusting that many people would benefit from it for years to come.

1

The following night, all the pupils returned to the secluded place on the edge of town, where the wise elder waited. He slowly turned his head, focusing his stare on each of their faces. He seemed upset.

Speaking intently, he said, "You have all returned to be initiated by me. Yet, today I discovered that two of you dared to break the vow of secrecy and told everyone in the village the sacred mantra!"

The two friends looked down at the dirt beneath their feet. It was clear to everyone else they were the guilty ones who broke the vow.

"I want those of you who kept the mantra a secret to leave now. I will fetch you later." He pointed at the other two, demanding, "Don't leave. For every action, there is a consequence." The man and woman trembled yet still felt sure they had done the right thing.

When the other pupils were out of sight, his face softened, and they saw a tear drop from the corner of one of his eyes. He stepped toward them and raised his arms to embrace them at the same time, whispering, "Thank you." He stepped back to face them again and continued, "I have traveled this land for many years, looking for those whom I could trust with this knowledge. Yet, none have passed the test. To my relief, the day has finally come. The two of you have passed the test. Because of your compassion, you were willing to help people everywhere by sharing the secret mantra, no matter the cost."

The two friends were stunned. They had not expected this kind of response.

The elder bowed to them graciously. Straightening up, he said, "The knowledge is yours now. And, it belongs to everyone. It always has. Your job is to remind the people what is already inside of them. Their potential is waiting to be re-discovered."

With that, he turned and disappeared into the forest, never to be seen again. The two friends joyfully returned to the village to continue what they had begun.

This story is how I think of Rob Freeman and Wendy Gallant. I learned who they were one fortunate day while browsing the internet for information about seeing without one's eyes. I was on a search.

Several years ago, I read a journal article from the Society for Scientific Exploration[1]. It described experiments in which children from China read short words written inside folded pieces of paper. These papers were tucked into their ears, their armpits, or otherwise hidden from plain

---

[1] Shen, Dong. (2010). Unexpected Behavior of Matter in Conjunction with Human Consciousness. *Journal of Scientific Exploration*. Volume 24(1). https://www.scientificexploration.org/journal/volume-24-number-1-2010

sight. Some of them were eventually trained to cut small pieces of wood or break strands of wire hidden inside containers, using only their minds. A few could even teleport small objects out from those containers.

At this time in my life, I had some breathing room after finishing another book and other projects and thought I would look into the matter of seeing without eyes, which I refer to here as "Mind Sight." I began to train myself using everything I'd learned over years of meditation and practicing telekinesis and other psychic abilities. At the time, I didn't understand that developing this ability could take much longer than the others had, and I began to look around for ways to learn it faster.

It was relatively easy to do an online search and learn about week-long training programs in Europe, Australia, and elsewhere. The combined course fees and travel expenses placed these out of reach for me. I also noticed that some of them required students to sign non-disclosure agreements. My nature has always been to teach others everything I learn myself, so I balked at the idea of being restrained from sharing what I learned at these programs.

Happily, I found the YouTube videos of Rob and Wendy being trained to see shapes, identify playing cards, and read letters. Their instructors were Nikolay Denisov[2] and Marina Kapirova from Russia. They had recorded a whole month of their training sessions and made them available for anyone to watch.[3]

Then, I found another of their channels[4] filled with videos of Rob and Wendy coaching each other to perceive colors. They used paper as well as three-dimensional objects.

Immediately, I noticed something special about them. They don't struggle. Instead, they play. They encourage each other. Positivity abounds in Rob and Wendy's sessions, as they express their joy and amazement openly, without hesitation. Their creativity produces exercises that abate any boredom.

What I say next is meant as the highest compliment. During their sessions, they become like children. They know how to decondition their minds from adulthood's limited way of perceiving, filtering, organizing, and

---

[2] See Denisov's site http://denisov-goldray.ru/ (Google can translate the page into English for you after you click any of the links)

[3] YouTube channel "Seeing Blindfolded Training-Wendy Gallant"

[4] YouTube channel "Seeing Blindfolded Practice - Rob Freeman"

ignoring aspects of our world. And I believe this is why they have succeeded in learning and teaching this ability.

The other reason they have been so successful is their perseverance. In this sense, adulthood offers its benefits. These are the development of grit and the understanding that results come from the continued application of effort over time. As of this writing, Rob and Wendy have been patiently and diligently training themselves for four years. These days, this type of commitment is rare even in adults. They set a crucial example.

And it is not without its risks. If their experience has been anything like mine, they have sometimes received unfair, ignorant, and hurtful comments from armchair critics and pseudo-skeptics. Fortunately, it seems people worldwide are succeeding at seeing without eyes with the help of their videos, which is evidence enough that this is real.

As with other controversial human abilities, non-believers cannot be convinced by debate or arguing. Having their own experiences is the only way to truly change their minds. But, few are willing to try. They see the videos and scoff. Yet, I and a growing number of people see Rob and Wendy at play and recognize that we are witnessing something genuine, enriching, intelligent, empowering, and life-changing.

I dedicate this book to Rob Freeman and Wendy Gallant in gratitude for their hard work. Instead of holding the knowledge inside of closed fists, their hands are open for all to see. And to hold. They are by no means finished, and I look forward to seeing what they do next.[5]

Rob Freeman

Wendy Gallant

---

[5] You can learn from Rob and Wendy too, and find a training partner, in their Facebook groups, "Learning To See Blindfolded - Rob Freeman" and "Blindfold Seeing/Consciousness/Energy/Psychic Abilities/CE5 Group"

Other teachers have come before, and without them, we might not know of this ability today. Lloyd F. Hopkins published his *Introduction to Mind Sight and Perception Research* in 1985 (printed as *Mind Sight and Perception*[6] in 1988). He was rejected from his church by its elders because of his work.

Jules Romains (born Louis Farigoule) published his *La Vision extra-rétinienne et le sense paratique; recherches de psycho-physiologie expérimentale et de physiologie histologique*[7] in 1921. The English translation is titled *Eyeless Sight*. His book was ridiculed, and Romains was prevented from doing further research.

We owe a debt of gratitude to these authors, as well as the doctors, scientists, mystic healers, and psychics who have reported or performed this ability in centuries past. No doubt humans have been able to do this for much longer than that.

I also want to acknowledge and thank all the other teachers worldwide working with children and adults today. We should also recognize forward-thinking researchers like Dean Radin, Ph.D., and organizations like the Institute of Noetic Sciences[8], The Monroe Institute[9], and The Rhine Research Center[10] for their willingness to apply scientific rigor toward investigating the nature of consciousness.

On a more personal note, I also want to take this opportunity to thank my friends in Denver. Specifically, those who've explored various psychic abilities with me this year, 2021, allowing me to share our insights with others through our videos. You've bent bars of steel, seen the future, and read each other's minds. But your greatest powers are your friendship, trust, openness, and humor. Cheryl Macchia, Carol Casebeer, Jill Lowy, Michelle Cox, Kavan Ganapathy, Stacy Linrud, Birgit Halbreiter, and those who prefer to remain anonymous. And Dawn Kirkwood.

Cierra, at the very beginning of my journey, when I didn't believe my own eyes, you did. And that kept me going. I love you.

---

[6] Hopkins, L. F. (1988). *Mind Sight and Perception*. Valley Press. Washington.

[7] For the English translation, see: Romains, J. (1978). *Eyeless Sight*. Citadel Press. New Jersey.

[8] https://noetic.org/

[9] https://www.monroeinstitute.org/

[10] https://www.rhineonline.org/

# PART 1

# THE FOUNDATION

# INTRODUCTION

This book is intended to fill a gap for those interested in learning Mind Sight or who are already training themselves. Some of you may have taken a course in-person or online, while others are experimenting by yourselves at home. Like me, you may have been inspired by videos you've found online. Hopefully, you have found much guidance from people like Rob and Wendy.

Yet, no matter how much information is available from various sources, I often read the same questions in online posts:

- "How do I get started?"
- "Where do I begin?"
- "What kind of materials do I need?"
- "How long does this take to learn?"
- "Can adults do this too?"

It would be some time before I decided to answer those questions and consequently produce this training manual.

In 2020 I began to train myself in Mind Sight, and kept a detailed journal of my experiences and the various insights they produced. I wondered whether there would ever be a reason to share what I'd learned publicly or if this would remain a private endeavor.

As I mentioned in the Acknowledgments, I never took a course from anyone else. Just as when I learned how to do telekinesis (moving objects with the mind), lucid dreaming, out-of-body experiences, and remote viewing, I did so without surrendering my ability to freely share the knowledge I gained through my efforts.

But as time passed, I felt no particular urge to do anything to answer the questions above for anybody else. There were several reasons for this. The Covid-19 virus had firmly taken hold, draping a blanket of stress and anxiety over the entire globe. I felt the stress like everyone else. I also contracted the virus. Although it was not severe enough to risk my life, the effects were enough to exhaust me for several months. I had also begun a master's degree, which required a lot of time. When not in school, I worked (and still do) a regular job to pay the bills.

I also felt drained of all my energy for reasons I can't quite identify. Having written other books about psychic development, I would periodically be invited to an online interview or podcast. Each time, I felt drained for days at a time following these interviews. Friends have suggested the notion of energy loss due to "cords" connecting me to other people, "energy vampires," and not setting strong enough boundaries to protect myself. I'm undecided, but open to that idea. More than that, I suspect that years of teaching psychic development in person and pushing myself to develop my abilities privately had taken a toll on the subtle energetic level. I was exhausted, through and through.

I ignored my feelings as much as I could until a powerful event occurred. As I wrote about in my memoir *Renegade Mystic,*[11] I had recently taken an interest in UFOs due, initially, to my personal contact experiences. I believe these were provoked by my explorations with out-of-body experiences. At first, these occurred in the liminal spaces of consciousness, just beyond the physical realm. Then, one afternoon, I had my first daytime sighting while lying on a small hill next to my wife. This was followed by a weekend in 2019 with Ricardo González and Paola Harris in Crestone, Colorado. Our group of fifty people had several UFO sightings over those two nights.

In September of the following year, I went to one of my favorite places on Earth, Moab, Utah. By this time, I'd been training myself in Mind Sight on a regular basis, and writing down all my experiences. So, I took my training materials with me for a stay at a yurt surrounded by beautifully desolate scenery. My main goal was to get much needed rest by spending the long weekend practicing yoga and meditation in solitude. My other goal was to have another UFO contact experience by using what many people now call a "CE-5" protocol.

The following account of what happened is taken from my journal:

*"I did a sky-viewing session from around 10:00 pm to 11:00 pm, then went to sleep. Around 3:00 am, I was roused from sleep, and felt compelled to go outside and look at the sky again.*

*I lied down so that I'd face the northwest sky (partly to avoid the glare from the full moon). And then I applied the mind-protocol I tried earlier that night to "call them." And to put it simply, I saw three lights appear, one at a time, less than a minute apart from each other, each one started off as a pinpoint of light, then quickly expanded to send a very bright "pulse" in my direction, then disappeared.*

---

[11] The complete title is *Renegade Mystic: The Pursuit of Freedom Through Consciousness Exploration*

*I don't know if it was the same object all three times, and it just moved a little bit in the sky each time, or if it was three separate objects. Regardless, it was very similar to what I experienced in Crestone last year.*

*After going back to sleep (after seeing the UFOs at 3:00 am), I had a spontaneous out-of-body experience. As soon as I separated from my body, a man appeared and held me to the ground. I was scared at first, but quickly realized he was trying to take care of me. He hovered over me with his body, and I intuited that he was some kind of shaman or healer on "the other side."*

*I sensed he was concerned that my energy level was too low to handle whatever I might be exposed to that night while having my OBE. I'm not surprised, because my energy has been extremely low due to stress and other things. He was sending healing energy into my non-physical body to help me somehow."*

After the experience ended, I felt confused and disappointed. It's relatively easy to receive positive and affirming messages during what I regard as spiritual experiences. But this time, this non-physical being communicated concern for my current state of being, and a need for me to be protected from further loss of energy. Was he connected to the UFOs I'd seen in the middle of the night? I'm not sure. But I was able to admit to myself that I had been drained of energy for quite a long time. I even had to acknowledge I was putting too much pressure on myself to learn to see without my eyes. That pressure made everything more difficult.

I'm a bit stubborn, so I continued training and recording my experiences for several more months. And then I stopped. I stopped teaching, I stopped doing psychic exercises with my friends, I stopped doing interviews, and I stopped developing my own abilities. I was empty inside, and needed to take a careful look at myself.

I spent most of 2020 and the early months of 2021 focusing on my normal responsibilities as a graduate student and a husband, and finishing *Renegade Mystic*. The only self-development I did at that time was meditation. I did it with the intention of reversing any "energy leaks" in my system, cultivating new energy, and conserving it for my health.

For a while, I believed I was completely finished being involved in consciousness exploration and being public about it in any way. My priority was to focus on my long-term spiritual development, which didn't require any involvement with psychic phenomena. I thought I was done with all that, and felt satisfied with everything I'd experienced the last few years of my life.

But if there's anything constant in life, it's change. And by the summer of 2021, I'd recovered most of my normal energy on physical and subtle levels. Aside from meditation, I'd resumed exercising and spending a great deal more time walking in nature. I didn't know it, but on a deep level I was ready to "report for duty" to receive those sacred callings which we all heed at some point in our lives.

One night, while trying to fall asleep, concepts began to flood my conscious awareness, seemingly from nowhere. I tried to ignore them and fall back asleep, but was unable to. One idea followed a chain of ideas before it, and they began to cycle in and out of my awareness so I would not forget them. Hours passed this way, and I fell back to sleep out of sheer exhaustion.

The next day, I filled an entire whiteboard with the previous night's ideas, and saw that I was answering those questions which begin this chapter, "How might someone train themselves to see without their eyes in a systematic way? What are the steps?"

After a couple more restless nights of new influx, I'd filled a second whiteboard. The two boards contained the essential outline and training regimen for what would become this book.

I do not refer to myself as a "psychic," or as anything else in particular. I realized the folly of titles a long time ago, and avoid them as much as possible. And truly, I don't have any inborn advantages. Whether it was telekinesis, out-of-body travel, or any other type of consciousness exploration, I had to work hard for a long period of time before having my own experiences. But I believe that my difficulties in learning these abilities is what make me a pretty decent guide to others who want to learn them.

When a participant has trouble grasping a concept or shifting their state of mind to produce the desired effect, I can help them because I have known that difficulty myself. Most of the questions participants ask are questions I had to navigate myself at one point. I know how to teach, and it is my greatest joy.

So, when my energy levels recovered, I wasn't too surprised that my first inspiration was to write this book.

I have a duty to be honest with you and tell you that my training stopped while I was learning to discern large shapes. As a *practitioner* of Mind Sight, I am still a beginner. Now, you may feel tempted to toss this book in the garbage upon reading my admission, but that would be a mistake.

I have been teaching one form of consciousness development or another, including meditation, for nearly two decades. Teaching is a talent of its own, and that is what I'm bringing to the table with this book. I'm confident that by sharing my successes as well as my errors from training myself, you'll receive the benefit of time saved, and increased understanding about the phenomenon you're trying to experience.

Like you, I only have a certain number of hours in a day, month, and year, to do with as I please. I could've chosen to use that precious free time over the next few years to focus on my own training without sharing what I know with anyone. But instead, I'm using my available time to write this book now, and to get the information out to anyone who is interested so that their process may become a little easier. Maybe by sharing my mistakes, you won't have to go through them yourself.

I also believe that the techniques I used when working with colors and shapes are transferable to the latter stages of identifying letters and numbers.

Children learn this ability quite naturally. If a guide takes the right approach and understands the psychological needs and differences of children, Mind Sight comes easily and quickly to them compared to adults. Adult brains are different from those of children.

I would never suggest this book for a child. It is designed for adults. Although there are exceptions to the rule, it is generally accepted that learning Mind Sight as an adult requires a considerable amount of time, say months and even years. This book includes a training log with specific, daily exercises. There is enough material in it to last between one and three years. It is designed to help you maintain a steady pace over a long period of time. Adults can benefit from this approach, whereas children don't need it all.

It is important that you not be swayed by the videos you'll inevitably find online of adults exhibiting incredible talent in seeing without eyes. Some of them are naturally inclined to it, much like Olympic swimmers born with the ideal DNA and body shape for gliding through water.

Others have been working hard on an almost-daily basis for several years to be able to do what they do. But that fact is difficult to convey over video. Returning to the example of Olympic athletes, everyone watches the race in awe, without any recognition of the years of patient, diligent training it took for the athlete to perform this way.

If you don't understand or accept that this takes time, you will become frustrated and give up before your brain has been given the chance to form the connections necessary for your subtle perception to enter your conscious awareness.

But, if you can stick with it long enough to see, feel, and know that you're perceiving a particular color held before you, *without using your eyes*, that may provide the fuel of inspiration necessary to stay the course.

Please, do go ahead, and enjoy those videos of people doing incredible things while blindfolded. Their examples can serve as a tremendous source of inspiration for all of us, as long as we understand the hard work and investment of time that was required for them to do what they do. Also, I suggest you consider the Recommended Reading list at the end of this book.

Life-long meditators understand this concept very well. Over time, they surrender any desire for peak experiences, or even to achieve enlightenment. Their approach is to focus on one day at a time, being present here, and now, instead of looking into the future while hoping for results to arrive quickly.

Meditation is part of their daily routine, much like brushing their teeth, reading the news, or exercising. After years of steadily applying their chosen method of introspection, and without any obvious results along the way, they can look back and say, "Something's different now. All that meditation must've changed me somehow, and I didn't even notice."

Indeed, Mind Sight training has more to offer than seeing without eyes. I regard it as a type of meditation in itself. I have been surprised at how much I've learned about my psychological and emotional programming.

During your training, you'll learn to peer deeply into your mind. The insights you'll gain have the capacity to affect the rest of your life in how you treat yourself, and others. I believe the insights from Mind Sight training can make us all happier, more patient, and more perceptive to life itself.

I can't ask anyone to treat this as a spiritual endeavor. But, I don't mind admitting that it has that quality for me. Like other types of consciousness exploration, finding evidence for our profound interconnectedness is inevitable.

It's already inside of you. All you have to do is *not* give up.

A selfie taken at the yurt that weekend.

# HOW TO USE THIS BOOK

The first thing the reader should know is this process is designed for adults interested in self-training. Many of us are introverts or have schedules that make it difficult to commit to meeting a partner on a regular basis or want to remain private about their exploration. However, you'll quickly find ways to incorporate working with a partner or group.

If you are a parent interested in teaching your children or adolescents Mind Sight, the training schedule for the 14 phases is *not* for them. Their brains are different! However, you can learn how to do the exercises and simplify them. You'll have to become very sensitive to your child's levels of joy and stress and be ready to respond appropriately.

Are you excellent at providing consistent encouragement? Many professional child educators know how to do this. If it's not your strength, then that's something to consider. Regardless, I hope this training method serves as a resource.

In one sense, this book is experimental, which is why I refer to it as a "pilot program." Some of these techniques are commonly known, and others, some of which involve online materials, are unique. We won't know their overall efficacy until many people have applied themselves to the training and reported their results.

As such, each phase of the program concludes with a link to an online survey.[12] These surveys are your opportunity to let me know how far you've come, how long it took you, which techniques worked well for you, which didn't, and how you think I can improve them.

Since the entire program can last between one and three years, I intend to create a second edition sometime around the year 2025[13] incorporating everyone's feedback. There are 14 phases of training, therefore you will have 14 opportunities to share your experience with me.

---

[12] You'll be able to complete the survey anonymously if you prefer to remain private.

[13] If you're reading this sometime after 2025 and still no second edition exists, it means not enough readers reported their findings or completed a significant portion of the program. It might also mean that everyone was satisfied with the first edition.

## THE 14 PHASES

Phase 1: Color familiarization

Phase 2: Color perception and confirmation with varying sets of 2 colors

Phase 3: Same as Phase 2, but with sets of 3 colors

Phase 4: Same as Phase 2, but with sets of 5 colors

Phase 5: Perceiving and contrasting black and white in various forms

Phase 6: Black and white in distinct shapes

Phase 7: Shapes in various colors, solid and hollow

Phase 8: Numbers

Phase 9: Capital letters

Phase 10: Lower case letters

Phase 11: Associating capital letters with their lower case counterparts

Phase 12: All upper case words

Phase 13: All lower case words

Phase 14: Upper and lower case words

     As discussed later, boredom can pose a challenge to anyone applying themselves to Mind Sight, especially for those untrained at holding one's attention on a single object for an extended period, as in meditation. Boredom during a single session is a challenge. More importantly, boredom over several weeks or months is an even more significant obstacle.

     There are at least two possible solutions to this problem. The first is what I call "going rogue," and the second is "cross training" and using "boredom busters."

# GOING ROGUE[14]

Every set of exercises is designed in a particular order for a reason. For example, the first five exercises of Phase 1 progress in this way:

Day 1: Blue and Red
Day 2: Blue and White
Day 3: Blue and Green
Day 4: Blue and Yellow
Day 5: **Blue** and Black

You will notice that one aspect of the first five days is that one particular color is repeated. In the first five days, that color is blue. You'll get to know blue pretty well, and you'll also get to know how it contrasts will each of the other colors.

Now let's look at Day 6, which marks the beginning of focusing on the color white:

Day 6: White and **Blue**

Did you notice that the first color you'll contrast against white is blue? These transitions are *intentional* overlaps across stages. They're designed to reinforce your perceptual ability across stages of training. This style of reinforcement continues in one way or another throughout the 14 phases.

Yet, the matter of boredom remains. Some readers may quickly grow tired of focusing on blue or any other color for five days in a row. Or, you may be more interested in starting with shapes[15] instead.

How do you choose between trodding on a carefully prepared path and bushwhacking your way through? **Nobody but you** can know what the best approach is **for you**. Sticking with a plan takes grit and patience. But for the wrong type of person, too much of that is, well, *too much*. And for that person, it can quickly diminish results.

In the realm of consciousness exploration and spirituality, there's nothing I dislike more than dogma. I offer this program as a type of

---

[14] For this book, I define "going rogue" as being independently minded and finding your own way.

[15] In this case, I strongly recommend developing yourself with Phase 5, contrasting black and white, before starting on shapes.

scaffolding. It's intended as a map for developing yourself. Yet, the map is not the same as the destination. Therefore, please feel free to "go rogue" if it feels right for you.

And, after reading the map, you might want to redesign it to suit you better or fold it up for later. If you ever get lost, you can always pull it out of your bag, open it up, and find your bearings.

Please consider the following before going rogue. The 14 phases are designed to provoke the growth of neural connections in the brain. This requires the consistent application of effort in a particular task over time. Think of toddlers slowly learning to move their bodies to be able to walk. Their brains rapidly form connections to move their legs and find their balance. They try and fall over and over again in a consistent effort until their brains and bodies are sufficiently developed to stand up.[16]

Being too random in your approach may not offer enough positive stress on the brain *over time* to cause it to learn.


ROGUE FEEDBACK

If you go rogue but would still like to offer your insights and feedback, please track your training schedule using your own calendar. Then use the links below to submit your feedback:

After 30 training sessions: **www.learnmindsight.com/roguesurvey30.html**

After 180 training sessions: **www.learnmindsight.com/roguesurvey180.html**

After 360 training sessions: **www.learnmindsight.com/roguesurvey360.html**


## CROSS TRAINING AND BOREDOM BUSTERS

Periodically inserting "off-book" exercises into your schedule can keep the process enjoyable. It also challenges your mind in different *yet complementary* ways.

---

[16] This speed of neuronal development may be a clue as to why children learn Mind Sight much faster than adults. But the adult brain is still perfectly capable of forming new connections.

Phases 1 through 4 focus on colors including black and white, and Phase 5 focuses solely on black and white. The primary tool you'll use is in the form of colored paper or thin sheets of foam[17].

These phases involve holding and moving the paper or foam around your head and body while trying to perceive its color. During the familiarization stage, you will know what the color is ahead of time. Familiarization is about learning and sensitization. In the next stage, you'll challenge yourself to perceive the color and verify your accuracy after each card. I refer to colored paper, paper printouts, and foam cards alike as "**cards**" throughout the book.

You'll perceive a card, then verify it, then move on to the next card, all without removing your blindfold[18]. But using only cards will become boring.

The boredom busters below can add an element of novelty while focusing on perceiving colors.

## Same Exercise - Different Object

You would still follow the prescribed order of training, but instead of cards, you could use balls, solid-colored paper (gift) bags, plastic cups, flowers, balloons, etc. Feel free to get creative. What if you baked some sugar cookies and covered them with colored icing?

The procedure would vary slightly. The cards will be shuffled during the verification exercises. Balls, bags and cups however, will just be pushed about until you forget their order, thus randomizing them.

The process of reaching for the next object on the table adds a new challenge not available with the cards - that of locating objects in space or "hunting."

## Using a Partner

Of course, many people are learning Mind Sight in group training programs or with partners. Some do it in person, while others do it online. Partners and groups can integrate any of the exercises in this book.

Perhaps your spouse, roommate, or child would be willing to hold your cards or objects for you? With partner work, maintaining a sense of fun,

---

[17] A complete list of required materials is provided later in the book.

[18] You'll learn the method for verification (without looking) later in the book.

relaxation, and positive encouragement is tantamount. If it feels like they're testing you or judging you, it won't work very well.

Ask them to behave as your cheerleader rather than your coach. Their feedback, including what they notice about you during your process, should serve as positive and constructive insights. This is not their opportunity to accrue a list of your faults.

Still, your partner will need to tell you whether your perception is accurate or not. If you say "It's blue" and it's another color, your partner can ask, "Please try again." or "Did you perceive anything besides blue?" or something similar.

Responding with "Wrong!" or making an annoying sound like what you hear on a game show or a videogame should be avoided. The slightest negativity can significantly reduce one's ability. Remember, we're nurturing *extreme sensitivity*. Mind Sight is an emotional process as much as a physiological, psychological, or even a psychic one. If your partner is a brute, stop working with them unless they're willing to change. If you're a brute to yourself, identify that tendency and strive to develop self-compassion.

See the example of partners working in person and by video conferencing on the next page.

# Working with a Partner

One person can hold or move the card near their partner's "windows" of perception.

Partners can also train using video conferencing technology. This style of training was pioneered by Rob Freeman and Wendy Gallant as seen in their Facebook pages and YouTube channels.

## Environmental Perception

Once in a while, you might choose to exercise your perception by sitting down somewhere and taking in the environment. If your home has a window facing the sidewalk, you might sit there with your blindfold on and set your intention to perceive people as they walk nearby. If you have a private yard, you might sit in front of a tree or some flowers and become sensitive to their presence. In Denver, the Botanic Gardens offers various places to sit. There, one can be present to incredibly vivid and energized plants, trees, and flowers. The indoor tropical exhibit is my favorite.

Rather than focusing on a specific object, you might broaden your focus to perceive the whole scene around you. People have reported their vision spontaneously opening up to perceive their surroundings this way. As always, steadily apply yourself without demanding instant results. In time, you may have a spontaneous opening yourself.

Please do this exercise only in spaces where you are safe. The benefit to doing this in your home, your fenced yard, or a protected area like the Botanic Gardens is the feeling of safety. Feeling safe is essential to the process, and being protected from danger is most important to your person.

## Being Present to Animals

Do you have a dog at home? Or a cooperative cat[19]? If they're comfortable resting in your lap, you could practice perceiving them. Borrowing from many energy healing traditions, you might hold your hands over their bodies and sense their energy fields that way.

Or, if you have a fish tank with one or two fish inside, you could sit close to the tank and practice perceiving them. If they're the kind of fish that don't move around very much, you could start by feeling which side of the tank they're on or whether they're still or moving around. You could also experiment with doing this while the tank's light is on or off.

Whether you do this with dogs, cats, fish, horses, or other animals, you might alternate sensing them while unmasked (using your eyes) with doing it while blindfolded. While using your eyes, you can ask yourself, "What do I feel? What do I intuit? What kind of thoughts come up?"

This practice can become especially useful when your pet exhibits pain or illness since it might help you understand what's happening. Paying attention to them this way may provoke spontaneous energy healing. Of course, please don't wait to take them to the veterinarian.

---

[19] I know, I know. This is like asking if you own a unicorn. ☺

## Boredom Busters for Shapes, Letters, and Numbers

Visit your local children's bookstore and select some books about shapes, letters, and numbers. Ideally, the books would be of identical or similar size. One book would be specific to letters. The next would be specific to shapes, etc.

Your first sessions with these books could start by shuffling them while blindfolded, then flip through each, attempting to perceive what each contains.

Then place one to your left, saying "This is the one about numbers," one to the right, saying "This is the one about letters," and one in the middle, saying "This is the one about shapes." And then remove your blindfold to see how you did.

Once your accuracy is satisfactory to you, you could focus on one book at a time, randomly opening a page and placing your intention there, then checking after a few minutes.

## Cross Training with Psychic Abilities

One of the first psychic abilities I ever trained myself in was telekinesis. During that time, I discovered that it opened a door of possibilities. For one, synchronicities occurred at an astounding rate. For example, my wife and I began calling or texting each other within a second of each other, which may involve some degree of telepathy.

Training in lucid dreaming, out-of-body experiences, and remote viewing had similar effects. One ability or experience can nurture another because they all arise from the same source, your mind.
Training in these abilities also opened the door for my contact with non-human or extra-terrestrial beings, which I believe is also a form of consciousness development.

Therefore, you might consider engaging in an adjunct path by training in psychic abilities. Be careful to do it as a periodic insertion into your Mind Sight training schedule. Don't let it replace it or diminish the positive stress from whatever Mind Sight phase you're focused on at the time. This is assuming that Mind Sight is still your priority. If you get more interested in something else, then naturally, you must follow your passion.

Of all my books, *Signal and Noise* is a good starting point, and it's filled with many exercises related to clairvoyance. But it can be helpful to consider a wide range of trainers and authors, so look around and see what other resources appeal to you. There might be people in your city offering half-day or weekend classes at a metaphysical bookstore or spiritual center. Or *you* could even start your own group! Meeting people with similar interests can feel very supportive and energizing.

Other forms of cross training will be discussed in Part 2, Across Space and Time, related to precognition, retrocognition, long-distance perception and other psychic modalities.

## IT'S ALL RIGHT TO STOP ANY TIME

When is enough, enough? One answer is, "When you've satisfied your curiosity." If you get halfway through Phase 1 and succeed, even just a little bit, you might feel completely satisfied with your exploration of Mind Sight and decide to stop. And that's completely valid.

Many of us are what career coach Barbara Sher referred to as "scanners" in her book *Refuse to Choose.*[20] Scanners are like honeybees. They linger at a flower just long enough to get what they need and then move on. Scanners are also fast learners. People judge them from leaving jobs or projects too soon or undone, not understanding that the scanner is satisfied and their task is complete *for them.*

Another answer is, "When you're beating yourself up or frustrated." There is no way to know how long it will take a person to succeed at any phase. One thing is for sure, the access to one's subtle mind suffers under duress. If you are hard on yourself, forceful, impatient, or looking to blame yourself or someone else, then it's time to stop. None of those behaviors will lead you toward success. At least, you should take a good long break and review your motivation before re-engaging this training.

The only reason to do it is to make yourself happy. And if you don't feel happy during the process, you won't end up happy in the end. I'm not writing this as a value statement about you. There's nothing wrong with you. It's just that your attitude may need adjusting, and maybe it's more about other parts of your life than this activity.

This brings us to stress. There is apparent stress and invisible stress. Apparent stress is when you *know* you're angry at someone, or frustrated with your job, or you're physically sick, or someone close to you has recently died.

---

[20] Sher, Barbara. (2007). *Refuse to Choose: Use All of Your Interests, Passions, and Hobbies to Create the Life and Career of Your Dreams.* Rodale Books.

Invisible stress is all around us. Think of the Covid-19 epidemic. It has worn us all down, even though Covid-19 itself is not perceptible to the eye. But changing regulations, changing workplaces, changing access to food and restaurants, the fear of contracting the virus, inability to gather or travel, etc., are ever-present factors. Even if you don't think you're affected by it, it has involved most people in your community, and *their state of mind affects yours.*

Don't we all experience times in our lives when apparent and invisible stressors wear us down? These are great times to take a break from unnecessary activities, including practicing Mind Sight. It could be an excellent opportunity to spend your free time every day practicing simple meditation, walking in the park (unplugged), or revisiting old episodes of wonderful shows like *The Great British Baking Show*, a personal favorite.

Consider fasting from social media and online news. It could also be worthwhile to see a counselor or therapist.

## FOR TEACHERS

Please feel free to use any concepts you find here in your teaching. There's no need to credit me in any way. And, if you have helpful suggestions for the next edition based on your experience teaching others how to see without eyes, I'd be interested in hearing from you.

If you wish to sell copies of this book during your programs, your local independent bookstore can order copies at a wholesale discount from INGRAM. All they need is the ISBN number, which is 978-1-7352930-4-2. Ask them for a price reduction for large orders.

Please don't photocopy or scan this book, or publish the web links. The book's sales income is used to pay for the annual website expenses.

You're **welcome to** print out the shapes, letters, numbers, and words to share with your students. You may also share the downloadable meditations with them.

## WHAT YOU SAY MATTERS

Books like this live and die by online reviews. Some people feel driven to post ignorant, aggressive, or unfair reviews for all to see, with the sole purpose of causing damage or suppressing information.

What you say matters in more ways than one. Whether you engage in the training or not, yes, please **do** post an online review about this book. It will help others when you are specific about how much of it you read and whether or not you engaged in the training. If you did train, how many sessions did you do? How long did you stick with it? What were the key reasons for your level of success?

Potential readers are savvy when scanning book reviews. They can differentiate between a biased pseudo-skeptic with an unscrupulous agenda and an earnest trainee who honestly and diligently applied themselves to the program.

So, if it matters to you to get this information out into the world, please post your review. Also, you might visit your local brick-and-mortar bookstore or library and ask them to carry this book on their shelves.

Thank you for your support.

# CONCEPTS AND QUESTIONS

## GET YOUR "THINKING" OVER WITH BEFORE TRAINING

Let me begin with an example from teaching telekinesis in the classroom. I can always tell which students will have the most difficulty moving their objects with their minds. They're usually the most educated people in the room, such as engineers and scientists. I can see their faces and guess what's happening inside their heads as they strain to produce the desired effect.

They're *thinking* about it.

They're trying to figure out *how* it works. Unfortunately, this cogitation prevents the deep state of physical and mental relaxation necessary for success.

Everyone else is in a state of flow and forming an effective connection with their objects. They're not trying to figure out the mechanism for this psychic effect. They're not contemplating quantum physics. Instead, they're present to the subtle impressions arising within their consciousness.

Whenever I notice the smarties struggling, I chat with them and confirm my suspicions. After I encourage them to reserve their analysis for after the class, they *let go* and eventually succeed after another period of relaxation.

The point is, this section contains topics for you to think about before or after training, not during. When you put on your blindfold and begin Phase 1, you'll need to pay attention to your *perceptions* and avoid focusing on your *thoughts*.

Have you ever driven along a highway and, several miles later, realized that you didn't notice anything because you were daydreaming? The same thing can happen during a Mind Sight training session. You can pass a whole hour ignoring valuable glimmers of experience because you were focused on your thoughts and analysis.

Once you put on your blindfold, forget about everything you've read in this book or learned from other sources. Just relax and perceive. You must be fully present with what is happening "here and now" once your blindfold is on. However, this is training advice for *beginners*. In time, you'll be able to see without eyes while thinking and talking at the same time.

# HOW DOES MIND SIGHT WORK?

Probably, the most common question people ask when beginning their training is, "How can a person see without using their eyes?" It is a perfect example of the thinking-style that should be reserved for before or after each training session, not *during* it.

Do you need to be a mechanical engineer to start your car and drive to your next destination? Do you need to understand hydrodynamics to enjoy kayaking? More to the point, our bodies breathe, heal, and digest without our knowledge of those processes. It's automatic.

One physical description for Mind Sight is "dermo-optical perception." The concept is that one's skin is capable of perceiving visual stimuli. Many videos from India feature children engaged in "midbrain activation"[21] and learning to see without eyes. They're seen rubbing colored paper up and down their arms and pressing them against their cheeks and foreheads, and even smelling them, then correctly determining the color.

In 1941, German troops invaded the Russian city of Leningrad. A 14-year old girl named Nelya Mikhailova[22], like other children had become a soldier. Nelya served as a radio operator inside a *tank*. Still a soldier several years later, she was injured by artillery fire and sent to recover in a hospital. While there, she spent time doing embroidery. At one point, she realized she could reach inside a bag holding various colors of thread and choose the one she wanted without looking inside. She could *feel* each thread's color.[23] Throughout the rest of her life, she would be known for a range of powerful psychic abilities, particularly telekinesis.

One day, when I had just begun training myself, I invited my wife to play with a stack of red and yellow cards and see if she could tell the difference between them. Having worked as a massage therapist for many years, she knew she could rely on the increased sensitivity in her fingers and palms. She held each card in one hand while hovering her other hand above it as if to *feel* the energy emanating from the card. Her accuracy indicated

---

[21] Midbrain activation training in India is highly controversial, partly because franchises of children's programs have sprouted everywhere. Education there is highly valued, and these programs advertise giving children a special advantage for learning.

[22] Mikhailova is famously known as Nina Kulagina.

[23] Ostrander, S., & Schroeder, L. (1970). *Psychic Discoveries Behind the Iron Curtain.* Prentice Hall.

she could indeed *feel* the difference between the red and yellow cards without touching them.

There are also cases of people using hypnosis to see with their fingertips or their cheeks.[24]

All of this is to say, one way Mind Sight is possible is by dermo-optical perception. Somehow, the brain can translate the information received through the skin and nervous system into visual imagery.

If you find this difficult to believe, consider the Brainport V100.[25] A visually impaired user wears a pair of sunglasses with a small camera attached to them. The camera is connected to a small computer. That computer is also connected to a device that is pressed against the user's tongue. Imagery from the camera is converted into electrical signals felt by the tongue. With practice, the user's brain learns to convert those signals into a visual image.

The tongue is a particularly sensitive organ. But do you know what the largest organ is? Your skin. And thanks to your nervous system, there's no need for wires and computer chips to communicate with your brain. Mother Nature's network only needs time to learn a new ability.

As an important aside, one may ask why more research into *natural* seeing without eyes hasn't been done. One reason is, by using one's innate abilities, there's no product to sell. Thus, no profit. On the other hand, developing artificial technologies has the potential for significant financial gain.

But is dermo-optical perception the *only* way a person can see without their eyes? No.

Many practitioners can perceive a target beyond visual range, for example, in another room. With the door closed, light cannot travel from the card to the person's skin. Yet, they can still perceive it accurately.

And what of the use of precognition and telepathy? These abilities are based on a target being separated from the person in both space and time. This indicates perception occurring via non-ordinary means, through one's consciousness. Of course, the body is always involved since non-physical consciousness expresses itself by interacting with the physical brain and body.

There are multiple possibilities for how it works. But ultimately, you don't need to know *how* it happens in order to *make* it happen.

---

[24] Leslie Shepard wrote a "new introduction" to Jules Romains' *Eyeless Sight* (see Recommended Reading). It includes a survey of dermo-optical perception.

[25] The Chicago Lighthouse. (n.d.). Brainport V100. *Tools for Living*. https://www.lighthousetoolsforliving.com/Brainport-V100_p_1554.html

# THE CONSCIOUSNESS CONNECTION

Earlier, we distinguished between dermo-optical perception and psychic, or "raw consciousness" perception. One is based on physical experience, while the other seems to transcend physical limitations. But is it accurate to label a consciousness experience *non-physical*?

One way to answer this question is to contrast Mind Sight with other non-ordinary states of perception and distant influencing.

Out-of-body experiences (OBEs) offer a good starting point. When people have OBEs, it is common to feel as if they're separating from their bodies. Or sometimes they suddenly appear in a different place without any sense of traveling there. Generally, it feels like the part of them that gives that sense of "me-ness" is wholly separated from the physical body. "I" am over here, and my body is "over there." But is that the case every time?

I've experienced OBEs simultaneously with dreams. In them, a dream scene was "playing" over my visual field, much like a "heads up display" (HUD) projecting information on a high-tech vehicle's front windshield.

The dream state occurs during a specific stage of sleep called "rapid-eye-movement" (REM). Dreams do not happen during the deepest stages of sleep when the brain is mainly producing delta-frequency brainwaves.

The point is, during my experience above, I perceived a brain-generated experience (a dream) at the same time as feeling as if I was outside of my body. Here, I'm implying that I was outside of my *brain*. So, even though I felt like I was entirely out of my body, is it possible that my brain was still involved in *processing* the experience? Or, did a portion of "me" remain in my body while the rest flew about in another reality? *Where is the windshield?*[26]

Dr. Eben Alexander offers a different possibility in his book *Proof of Heaven: A Neurosurgeon's Journey into the Afterlife.*[27] His is a story of an unintended Out-of-Body Experience, in the form of a Near Death Experience. In his case, the part of his brain that could reflect or produce conscious experience was completely off-line due to a severe bacterial

---

[26] Congenitally blind people can "see" during OBEs and NDEs. See Kenneth Ring's book, *Mindsight: Near-Death and Out-of-Body Experiences in the Blind* (see Recommended Reading)

[27] Alexander, Eben. (2012). *Proof of Heaven: A Neurosurgeon's Journey into the Afterlife.* Simon and Schuster.

meningitis infection. He spent several days in a coma. Yet, he was wide awake and fully aware in another realm, "the afterlife."

In his case, it seems his brain was *not* necessary for his experience of non-physical consciousness. Needless to say, though, his brain *was* necessary for him to use his voice to share his experience with us afterward.

Researcher Grant Cameron interviewed psychic teacher Leonie Appelt and her grandson, Seth. Leonie has trained Seth to see without his eyes to such a degree that he can drive a car that way. During the interview[28], Grant asked them to describe what it's like for Seth. He replied, "It's like your spirit is, like, popping out of your head and having a look around."

It seems that for Seth, seeing without eyes is sometimes like having an OBE while simultaneously being present in the body. It isn't surprising, given that marathon runners, women giving birth, and people experiencing trauma have reported leaving their bodies while remaining awake and conscious.

We should note something interesting about the runners, mothers, and terrified experiencers. In each case, we can assume their bodies are in a state of exertion. And their breathing pattern matches that state.

When I taught myself how to do telekinesis, I relied on my previous training in meditation. I knew that *how* a person breathes could affect their mind and their flow of internal energy. Practitioners of Chi Kung, Hatha Yoga and other energy-based disciplines know this well. When I breathed a certain way, I relaxed my body and mind to the degree that it felt like energy was flowing through me and beyond me.

Wide awake and fully conscious, albeit in an altered state, I could move very light objects using my mental and energetic states. Yet, those effects relied on my first reaching the appropriate physical state.

It is unnecessary to decide whether consciousness operates completely separate from the nervous system or not. Some people's experiences suggest that it can.[29] Every experience is likely unique, and the

---

[28] Grant Cameron Whitehouse UFO. (2021, August 5). YouTube. *Grant Cameron on Blindfold Discussion with Leonie Appelt and Seth, and Wendy Gallant.* https://www.youtube.com/watch?v=QNWEsZfQmcw (at 25 minutes, 17 seconds).

[29] I should also note another possibility, although it's outside the scope of this book. Uri Geller's biography illustrates non-human intelligences, perhaps extra-terrestrial, influencing a human's capacity for psychic phenomena. I recommend his autobiography as well as Andrija Puharich's work, both listed in the Recommended Reading section.

underlying mechanism changes accordingly. As an anti-dogmatic person, I prefer to continue asking questions rather than pinning down what is most likely an incorrect explanation.

The point is that conditioning one's body through relaxation exercises influences one's state of consciousness. Therefore, when you begin Phase 1, it will be essential to incorporate the preparatory stages of relaxation and meditation rather than skip them. The more you condition your body, the easier it will be for your mind.

First, have your vegetables, then you can enjoy dessert.

A person may read this discussion about the physical brain and non-physical consciousness and exclaim, "Nonsense! I think out-of-body experiences, near-death experiences, and the rest of it are nothing more than hallucinations! There's no evidence that they're real!"

In response, I could suggest they read about "Miss Z," the subject of an OBE experiment discussed in Dr. Charles Tart's book, *The End of Materialism*.[30] She was able to read hidden numbers while traveling outside her body. The numbers were verified after she returned and reported her experience to the scientist.

But, I think it's more fun and impactful to tell that person the experience we're having at this moment while we're alert and awake in our bodies *is a hallucination*.

Have you heard this one before? "If a tree falls in the forest, and nobody's there to hear it, does it still make a sound?"

The answer is, "No, it does not make a sound." The reason for that is for humans and other creatures, *sound does not exist* outside the brain. Sound occurs when vibrations stimulate the ear, sending signals to the auditory cortexes of the brain in the temporal lobes. They create an auditory hallucination for us to experience within our consciousness.[31]

What about sight? Is sight just a hallucination? Yes. Vision occurs when photons enter the eyes, stimulate the rods and cones (photoreceptors), sending information through the optical nerve into the parts of the brain responsible for vision. There, we hallucinate colors and depth, giving us our three-dimensional experience of space and objects.

Let us revisit the question, "How does Mind Sight work?" If the mechanism is dermo-optical perception, our brain will interpret signals from

---

[30] Tart, Charles T. (2009). *The End of Materialism: How Evidence of the Paranormal Is Bringing Science and Spirit Together*. New Harbinger Publications

[31] For a fascinating and easy-to-read book about the brain and perception, I recommend *The Brain: The Story of You*, by David Eagleman.

our skin to produce visual hallucinations of color and depth. The process mimics that of our eyes.

Suppose we use raw consciousness instead of dermo-optical perception, for example, to see a target in another room. In that case, our consciousness *directly* stimulates the brain to produce the hallucination of vision.

Whether using dermo-optical perception or raw consciousness, we're trying to provoke "synesthesia". Around 2% of people naturally experience it and do things like taste shapes or see numbers as having specific colors.

Hallucinogenic drugs can temporarily induce synesthesia.[32] This implies that the brain temporarily changes how it processes information. I don't advise using mind-altering substances, especially for Mind Sight.

So, what can we do?

Children's brains offer us a clue. For adults, the "theta" brainwave state is associated with "internal focus, meditation, prayer, and spiritual awareness. It reflects the state between wakefulness and sleep and relates to the subconscious mind" (Neurohealth, n.d.)[33]. So, for adults, theta is a special state achieved through intention while awake or by relaxing while falling asleep. But, it occurs naturally in children while they are wide awake!

That's why I hypothesize that when a seer's[34] training includes inducing the theta state through relaxation, meditation, and similar activities, it increases their potential for temporary synesthesia.

This is a possible explanation for why a seer may sometimes "hear" the color. The brain translates the experience as "blue," but instead of creating a visual hallucination, it uses language. Even more subtle, your brain may create the experience of *knowing.* You *just know* it's blue.[35]

The only question left is, "Do you trust your inner experience?"

---

[32] Carpenter, Siri. (2001, March). Everyday Fantasia: The World of Synesthesia. *American Psychological Association*, 32(3). https://www.apa.org/monitor/mar01/synesthesia

[33] Neurohealth. (n.d.). https://nhahealth.com/brainwaves-the-language/
[34] From this point on, I'll refer to practitioners of Mind Sight as "seers."

[35] For this reason, "Mind Sight" is a misnomer, as is "seeing without eyes" and the other titles referring exclusively to vision. A more accurate name would be "Mind *Perception*." Frankly, it just doesn't roll off the tongue. And except for people who are visually impaired, we tend to use vision more than other sense to make our way in the world.

# CAN I *REALLY* LEARN TO DO THIS?

How do you think of yourself? If you don't experience Mind Sight the first time you try it, will you say to yourself, "I guess I'm one of those people who can't do it."? Or will you tell yourself, "That's alright. I just need to keep working at it and eventually I'll experience Mind Sight."

If you answered the first way, that you're "just not one of those people," then you've described yourself as someone having what Dr. Carol Dweck calls a "fixed mindset."[36]

If instead, you answered, "If I keep trying, I'll get there," then you've got what Dr. Dweck calls a "growth mindset."

People with a fixed mindset are driven to prove themselves over and over again. They want to show they're doing the most possible with the limited amount of resources with which they've been endowed.

Those with a growth mindset, however, believe one's potential is unknown and possibly unlimited. For them, life isn't a test but rather an exploration. Failures aren't failures to them. They're just learning lessons and growth opportunities.

I believe a reader with a growth mindset will have a more successful time learning Mind Sight than one with a fixed mindset because:

1.  They won't give up right away.

2.  They'll treat each session like a game or an adventure rather than a test or evaluation.

3.  They won't be driven anxiously by the need to prove their abilities to others.

You might memorize the three factors listed above. They'll keep your approach on the right track throughout all the phases of training.[37]

Be a *friend* to yourself.

---

[36] Dweck, Carol S. (2007). *Mindset: The New Psychology of Success.* Ballantine Books.

[37] I also recommend *Drive: The Surprising Truth About What Motivates Us* by Daniel H. Pink, as well as *Grit: The Power of Passion and Perseverance* by Angela Duckworth.

# AVOID THE DECLINE EFFECT

When I work with friends in Denver or teach remote viewing classes to the public, I often use lottery numbers as targets for precognition[38]. Unfortunately, strangers misunderstand our intention as chasing after money. The fact is, the lottery serves two purposes.

First, it's an ideal random number generator. It would be less random if I, as the group leader, selected those numbers myself. Why should the students see the numbers in the future using precognition? They could read them from my mind using telepathy instead.

By using the lottery, no person selects the numbers. This removes the possibility of telepathy. Until we check the winning numbers on the lottery's website, no one has a way of knowing them by ordinary means.

Second, and perhaps more importantly, using the lottery adds the element of *fun* to the process.[39] Fun is stimulating. Fun is captivating. Fun is energizing. Also, fun eliminates self-consciousness and hesitation. Without fun, these experiments become boring. As parapsychologists are well aware, boredom leads to the "decline effect."

In the 1930s, Joseph Banks Rhine researched psychic abilities in the laboratory. At first, the subjects performed well. But over time, their accuracy declined, and he realized their tasks had become monotonous. On some level, their minds had become disinterested in performing boring psychic tasks over and over again. Thus, the term "decline effect."

You will need to guard against the decline effect from Phase 1 to Phase 14 if you choose to go that far. You'll need to find methods to stimulate emotional engagement whenever you notice boredom setting in. Inserting boredom busters and cross training into your weekly schedule will help with that. Avoiding overtraining by taking time off once in a while will also help. Working with a partner or a group will also contribute a sense of novelty[40] and positive challenge.

---

[38] Working as a team, we used Associative Remote Viewing to predict the Colorado Pick 3 lottery twice in 2019 correctly and came close many other times. The details, photos, and transcripts are in my book *Signal and Noise*.

[39] You will learn an experimental method to predict lottery numbers using pregocnitive Mind Sight later in this book.

[40] Here, novelty is defined as being "new or unusual." Merriam-Webster.

# TO BECOME LIKE CHILDREN

Children learn to see without their eyes very quickly, often within one or more days. Some adults may have a similar experience, but more often I hear of them requiring months and years of steady practice. Why the difference?

In a 1999 press release from UC Berkley, Patricia McBroom discussed a book titled *The Scientist in the Crib: What Early Learning Tells Us About the Mind*[41] written by Alison Gopnik Ph.D. and others.

She wrote, "Before preschoolers enter kindergarten, their brains are more active and more flexible, with more connections per brain cell, than the brains of adult human beings... By age three, the child's brain is actually twice as active as an adult's. It has some 15,000 synapses or connections per neuron, many more than in the adult brain."[42]

Children's brains learn at a much faster rate than of adults. Among other things, they're growing neural connections related to the sense perceptions of sight, sound, smell, taste, and touch and how the rest of the brain relates to those senses. It seems feasible to assume their brains can just as easily grow neurons to develop dermo-optical perception or even raw consciousness perception.[43]

Adults don't have a way to turn back the clock and grow their brains at a child's pace. Fortunately, children possess pro-learning attributes that adults can also experience. These attributes positively impact an adult's process of learning Mind Sight.

First, children who are well-nourished, physically and emotionally safe and cared for, and loved, are relatively free of negative and chronic stress.

---

[41] Gopnik, Alison, Meltzoff, Andrew N., Kuhl, Patricia K., et al. (2000). *The Scientist in the Crib: What Early Learning Tells Us About the Mind*. William Morrow Paperbacks.

[42] McBroom, Patricia. (1999, August 10). *In the new science of children's minds, babies are smarter than adults, according to book co-authored by UC Berkeley psychologist.* University of California, Berkley. https://www.berkeley.edu/news/media/releases/99legacy/8-10-1999.html

[43] Unfortunately, a discussion about children with psychic abilities is beyond the scope of this book.

On the other hand, adults regularly experience chronic and debilitating stress. We struggle with our jobs, money, relationships, traffic, politics, social media, etc. The responsibilities of adulthood weigh heavily on our shoulders.

I can say from personal experience that stress makes learning difficult, especially when it comes to developing psychic abilities. Whereas relaxation nourishes psychic development, stress is like kryptonite.

Therefore, an adult training in Mind Sight should prioritize cultivating a *stress-reducing lifestyle*. Stress reduction often relies more on reducing activities more than adding new ones. I suggest reducing time spent on the internet, especially watching the news and social media.

If you are a workaholic, spending less time at work could help. If you often seek the company of people who inevitably leave you feeling drained, it might be good to see them less often.

Or, your social calendar may be filled to the brim with various activities and time with friends. Even though these are positive activities, the requirement to keep a full schedule and arrive on time, every time, is a source of stress in itself. The point is, doing less of *everything* can naturally provide you with more space to breathe.

In terms of adding stress-reducing activities to your schedule, meditation is an excellent place to start. Meditation naturally promotes mental and physical relaxation. Relaxation, in turn, leads to stress reduction.

The other benefit of meditation training is it develops one's sensitivity to subtle mental experiences.

In the beginning, one's mind may resemble a stormy ocean whose turbulent waves, one's thoughts, obscure the water. But with practice, the storm passes, the sea becomes still, and the water becomes clear. At that point, the meditator can look into the depths and see what's happening below.

I hypothesize Mind Sight works by training the brain to translate subtle stimuli into sensory experiences. Whether these are signals from the skin due to dermo-optical perception or signals from consciousness itself doesn't matter. What matters is that we consciously notice the faint impressions we experience while wearing our blindfolds. *Noticing* them will stimulate the brain into learning how to *interpret* them.

But suppose our minds are unaccustomed to being present to subtle mental events. In that case, we'll quickly become distracted by wandering thoughts, daydreams, and worries. Glimmers of color and shadow will flash and disappear without our noticing them. Our brain might project the word "green" into our consciousness, but we're too busy thinking about some Facebook post or a recent workplace drama to notice it.

These subtle stimuli are valuable, and we don't want to miss them.

Energy-based practices like Chi Kung and Tai Chi offer the same benefits as meditation and incorporate bodily movement. Being energy-based, they provide the benefit of helping us become sensitive to subtle energy experiences.

Earlier in this book, I shared how my wife quickly discerned two colors of cards by feeling their energy with the palm of her hands. She was using a type of dermo-optical perception. And, it worked because she had trained herself to be sensitive. I wouldn't be surprised if Reiki and other energy healers are naturally proficient at Mind Sight, or at least fast learners.

Along with subtle energy, physical energy is vital. Think of children in the morning. They wake up too soon for their parents, bouncing off the walls, ready to explore the world. The biological fact is, the mitochondria in each of their cells are fully charged, efficiently converting food and oxygen into energy. For us adults, our aging mitochondria might not work as well.[44] And stress doesn't help.

Too many of us adults are exhausted at the end of the day because of stress. We feel tired all the time. And then we develop the habit of "resting" in front of the television or computer for hours on end. But that kind of "rest" doesn't invigorate us.

Instead, we can recharge our batteries by moving our bodies. Taking a long walk outside often makes me feel better than I would have had I taken an afternoon nap or drank coffee. A brisk walk on my treadmill makes me feel more refreshed afterward.

We need all the physical energy we have to keep from falling asleep during meditation and our Mind Sight sessions. We need it to stay inspired and create the time in our daily calendar to practice. Perhaps more importantly, our brains need the energy to grow the newly stimulated connections to produce Mind Sight.

There is another lesson we can take from children. Unlike stuffy adults, children express their emotions freely, without hesitation. When they're sad or angry, they cry. When they're happy, they laugh and smile. They don't waste any energy suppressing or misrepresenting their emotions the way adults do. They feel and express their emotions one hundred percent.

---

[44] Herpich, C., Franz K., Klaus S., et al. (2021, February). Age-related fatigue is associated with reduced mitochondrial function in peripheral blood mononuclear cells. *National Library of Medicine.* https://pubmed.ncbi.nlm.nih.gov/33279665/.

Adults, on the other hand, often suppress their feelings or lie about them. I wager the most common lie in technologically advanced countries is the response to the question, "How are you?" You know the lie. We say it every day.

"I'm fine."

Adults rely on a set of brain processes known as "executive functioning." This is higher-order processing involved in long-term thinking, planning, focus, and memory. It's also involved with self-regulation.[45] Whenever you suppress your emotions, you rely on your brain's executive functioning. And you're draining yourself of energy by doing so.

Your whole brain uses immense amounts of glucose to work, and executive functioning requires much of it. Suppressing your emotions is physically draining because of the energy it consumes.

And, *suppressing your emotions trains you to ignore the subtle experiences of your mind*. Unfortunately, this is the exact opposite of what's required to develop Mind Sight.

Therefore, I might suggest one more way to be as a child. Allow yourself to feel your heart. Find someone you can be honest with, and share your true feelings. It might be a friend or family member. It might also feel safer to try this with a licensed therapist or counselor. When you begin opening up this way, you may feel tired afterward. But if you stay open, that feeling will be replaced by a sense of renewal and replenishment.

Please allow me to end this section with a journal entry from my Mind Sight training:

*July 28, 2020*
*"A strange event. While working with the cards, I suddenly had a strong vision of standing in a room and looking at a baby in a crib. As I looked closer at the baby, I realized it was me. I could tell it was me because the shape of the skull was just like what I've seen in baby pictures. I haven't seen a baby picture of myself in many years, so I have no idea why this vision would flash into my mind, especially while doing this exercise."*

Sometimes anomalies occur during consciousness exploration. When this spontaneous vision came to me, I had no explanation for it. Now I wonder if this was a deeper part of me, like a "higher self", telling me to be like a child? Or could it have served as a marker, so that I would write this particular chapter in the future? There's no way to know for sure, but I'm satisfied at being able to ask the question.

---

[45] Honos-Webb, Lara. (2018). *Brain Hacks: Life-Changing Strategies to Improve Executive Functioning*. Althea Press.

# PREPARATORY EXERCISES

There is one more dimension to becoming like children. For them, the imaginal world is not separate from what we perceive by ordinary means. They have invisible friends. They see fairies. They recollect past lives.[46] They speak with the recently departed.  Their dreams are vivid.

Whether or not any of their experiences above are "real" or not doesn't matter for this discussion. What is important is that they display a high degree of sensitivity as well as strong *inner* perception. They see the objects inside their consciousness with clarity.

While I trained myself, I strove to understand how I might improve my visual perception. I realized that I needed to improve my *imagination*. Suppose the colors and shapes in my mind's eye were dim, blurred, or otherwise indistinct. Why should I expect new impressions from my training regimen to produce better images than those?

A direct way to ask the question above is, "How well can I see the color yellow *in my imagination* when my eyes are closed?"

Go ahead, try it now. Close your eyes for a few minutes, and try to see the color yellow in your mind's eye, your imagination. After imagining the color yellow for a minute or so, answer these questions:

- Could you see the actual color?

- How bright was is?

- How big was it?

- How clear was it?

- Was it just color, or did it have a shape or boundary?

Different people will have different experiences with this brief exercise. Some will barely perceive color within the darkness behind their closed eyes, while others will see it *as if* it was on paper in front of them. Visualization is important because your brain will use this ability to *translate* non-ordinary perceptions into imagery.

---

[46] See Episode 6 of the 2021 television series *Surviving Death*, directed by Ricki Stern and written by Leslie Kean, originally released on Netflix.

Please don't be discouraged if this exercise was difficult for you. The exercises below will help you improve over time. I recommend making them a regular part of your life, especially while training in Phases 1 through 4.

You might even spend a few days or weeks doing them before beginning Phase 1.


# DREAM RECOLLECTION

Dreams naturally blend reality with imagination. They often use our memory to create the scenes and situations which excite, puzzle, or terrify us in our sleep. When you wake up from a dream, how clear are the images you remember? Do you dream in color? Generally, while we're in the dream, we don't question the people, places, and things we perceive. But as soon as we wake up, we realize it was just an illusion, and it quickly fades away.

Improving our dream recollection is a wonderful way to improve our skills. It combines the use of memory, visualization, and doing it while in a relaxed state of mind.

There are three types of dream recollection: immediate, journaled, and when returning to sleep.

## Immediate Dream Recollection

This practice is done *immediately* after waking up from a dream. The longest rapid-eye-movement (REM)[47] periods occur in the last few sleep cycles, in the early morning hours and right before waking up. So, you can expect to have the best dreams on days you wake up naturally without an alarm clock. It's also possible to wake up in the middle of the night to use the bathroom and realize you were having a dream just then.

Immediately after waking up, recall as much of the dream as possible. Close your eyes and replay it several times. As you do, pay attention to the colors, and brighten them in your mind's eye. Make every aspect of the dream as clear and vivid as possible. In the beginning, it might help to choose only one aspect of the dream to work with. Choose an aspect that is easy to hold your attention to for several seconds at a time.

---

[47] We dream during the REM stage of sleep. We sleep in cycles ranging from 90 to 110 minutes, and each cycle includes some amount of REM. The longest REM periods, which produce the longest dreams, occur in the cycles before waking.

Here's a tip: It can be easier to hold a dream object in mind if you imagine it in motion instead of keeping it still. Did you dream of Uncle Ricardo wearing a red cowboy hat? While holding that image in mind, see him walking around so you see the hat shifting its position as he turns his head. It's easier to pay attention that way.

## Journaled Dream Recollection

Journaling your dreams is a powerful practice. If you open any book about lucid dreaming[48], you'll see "dream journaling" presented as the foundation for the practice. Dream journaling trains us to remember our dreams better.

It is common for a dreamer engaged in this practice to wake up and accurately remember two, three, or more dreams they had during the night. For a lucid dreamer, the point is to eventually recognize they're having a dream *while* the dream is still happening, thus becoming "lucid" at that point.

Once lucid, they can explore, play, and learn inside their dream environment. The first thing many lucid dreamers do is fly since in dreams, gravity is an illusion.

For a seer, the benefit of dream journaling is exercising one's memory of the dream. The act of writing down what you dreamed requires you to *apply sustained effort* in remembering. When we remember something, we visualize it. Remembering is visualizing.

All you need is a notebook and pen. Keep them on your bedside table and commit to writing down anything you remember as soon as you wake up.

I know some people will say, "I don't dream." But that is not true. The REM stage of sleep is part of every person's sleep cycle. What you really mean is, "I don't *remember* dreaming."

Fortunately, you don't need to have good dream recollection in order to start this practice. You see, your intention to record your dreams will kick off a process that, in time, will deliver brief glimpses of last night's events.

If you wake up and don't remember anything, write down, "I didn't remember anything from last night." Before you write that, though, close your eyes and dig deep. If you remember a mood, a theme, a feeling, or a word, anything, write it down. Keep at it, and over time you'll remember more and more.

---

[48] *Renegade Mystic* (2nd edition) includes a set of lucid dream instructions, as well as several of my personal journal entries.

If you wake up in the middle of the night and remember a dream but don't want to turn your light on to write, just scribble in the dark. It's more important to go through the process of remembering and writing it down than it is to be able to read your chicken scratch the next day.

Another tip: You may have changed your body's position in bed after waking up. If you're having trouble remembering your dream, move your body back into the position it was in when you were asleep, and relax. Then try to remember your dreams again. Memory is *physical* as well as mental.

Returning to Sleep

This practice relies on longer-term memory. After you've turned off the lights and lied down for a good night's sleep, spend a few minutes remembering last night's dream. This would be a lot easier if you journaled it this morning immediately after waking up. You could also read your journal entry a few times before turning off the light. Then, replay the dream in your mind as you fall asleep.

This is similar to a technique called "wake initiated lucid dreaming (WILD)." Sometimes a person wakes up in the middle of a REM stage. If they fall asleep right away, it's possible to return to that REM stage. And, if they happen to be visualizing (remembering) last night's dream while returning to REM, it can become an active dream. The difference is, they'll now be *aware* they're dreaming *while* they're dreaming.

For our purposes, we won't be concerned with returning to REM and becoming lucid. But don't be surprised if you accidentally become a lucid dreamer along the way.

Our goal is to strengthen our ability to perceive mental objects. By doing this in bed at night, we're naturally more open than during the day. We shift from a predominantly beta-wavelength brain state, which is very alert, to a relaxed alpha-wavelength before going even deeper into sleep.

# SPONTANEOUS DAYTIME EXERCISES

Another way to improve your visualization is by using your immediate environment. If you go for a walk outside, take a moment to look at the blue sky. Then, close your eyes and recreate the image of the blue sky, and enhance the blue. Try to make it as accurate and vivid as when you see the sky with your eyes open. Then, repeat the process after looking at green grass, a red fire hydrant, a yellow car, etc.

If you're having trouble with dream recollection, you can use your daytime visualizations instead. Recall the blue sky, green grass, and red fire hydrant as vividly as you can while relaxing in bed before drifting to sleep.

## GUIDED VISUALIZATIONS - COLOR IN CONTEXT

At a certain point, I became frustrated with trying to imagine colors. For example, I would lie in bed at night with the lights turned off and close my eyes, simply trying to see "red." Just the color, nothing else. Most of what I saw was the dark backdrop of my mind's eye, my mental screen. Any redness I could produce was dull and faint.

Then I realized I could see better by putting color in context. Another way to say it is by giving the color a boundary, an edge. Here's something you can try right now. Close your eyes, and see the color yellow. Try to hold that color for ten seconds.

How was your experience? Was it easy or difficult? Was the yellow bright and clear? Was it hard to hold on to? Or was it fully present the whole time?

Now try this. Do you remember the character Big Bird from Sesame Street? If you do, you can already see Big Bird's tall body covered in broad yellow feathers. The long beak is also yellow. You also see Big Bird's black and white googly eyes and long, orange legs.

Close your eyes and imagine Big Bird moving around and talking. You can probably hear Big Bird's voice as clearly as when you were a child.

Now, you've added *context* to the color yellow. The yellow has a border in this scene. The edge forms Big Bird's body's shape and contrasts with other colors and a sense of depth. Yellow is now much easier to perceive on your mental screen.

Remember this when beginning Phase 1, working with colored cards. Your intention should not only be to perceive each card's color but also the shape and boundary of the card. Since you'll be holding your cards, you'll be able to feel the edges, helping you create a mental image of the card's shape. Adding this context will make it easier to perceive the color itself.

I have recorded several guided visualizations for you to listen to. In them, you'll practice perceiving colors *in context* by imagining specific objects and scenes.

The guided visualizations can be found at **www.learnmindsight.com/preparation.html**

# GUIDED MEDITATIONS

I have also recorded a variety of guided meditations for you to listen to. I recommend listening to them while wearing your blindfold. They are designed to help you relax and become more sensitive to subtle experiences. The later phases of this program don't include a timing device or any kind of recording. Therefore, you might benefit from listening to one of these meditations before starting your session. Of course, you can use them any time to best suit your needs and preferences.

You can listen to these meditations at
**www.learnmindsight.com/preparation.html**

# THE COLOR WHEEL - REDUX

In his book *Mind Sight and Perception*, Lloyd Hopkins described a "Color Wheel," a training device he used with his students. The person would sit ten feet away from the wheel. The wheel was segmented into several colors. It is unclear from the reading whether the wheel was lit so that only one color would shine on the student or if another method was used.

After exposing the student to one of the colors, Hopkins would tell them the color so their mind, brain, and body could associate their perceptions with the stated color.

Hopkins wrote, "This association sets up flashes and patches of individual colors in the student's visual field" (Hopkins, p. 42).[49]

Inspired by his color wheel, I've created a digital version. It's not a wheel, though. Rather, it's a selection of videos that project solid colors onto the screen. At the same time, you'll hear my voice telling you what that color is.

In **Stage 1 of the color wheel**, you'll work with a single color at a time, alternating between closing and opening your eyes. This is the start of training your brain to associate how a color *feels* with what you see with your eyes. You should also spend time doing the same thing working with a color card. You might also listen to a guided meditation beforehand.

You might spend several days on a single color, sitting in front of the color wheel for half the session **and working with the same color *card* for the rest of your session**. See the chapter Working with Color for directions on working with a card.

---

[49] Hopkins, Lloyd F. (1988). *Mind Sight and Perception*. Valley Press.

In **Stage 2 of the color wheel**, the videos are more complex. You'll be blindfolded the whole time, and the colors will change. My voice will tell you what color you're seeing and alert you when a new one is *about* to appear. This will allow you to sense the change of color on your own. I'll also tell you when the color has changed, and what color it has changed to, so you won't be left wondering.

In **Stage 3 of the color wheel**, you'll be exposed to a color without being immediately told what it is. This will give you around 30 seconds to recognize and feel the color change. After 30 seconds, you'll hear me tell you that it has changed, and what color it changed to.

If possible, watch the "digital color wheel" from a large screen such as a laptop instead of your smartphone. And, if you can play it on a big-screen television, even better. **Turn off the lights and do this at night, so the room is darkened in order to experience the color as brilliantly as possible.**

Assuming dermo-optical perception is at work, do this practice while exposing as much skin as possible. Taking your shirt off is ideal if you're comfortable doing so. Otherwise, wear a tank top or short-sleeved shirt, exposing your neckline and shoulders as much as possible.

For Stage 1 as well as Stages 2 and 3, it will be important that you don't become passive while using the color wheel. While your eyes are closed, use your intention to *consciously* feel, or rather, perceive the color being projected.

It's possible to let an entire session pass by daydreaming about other things, thinking your skin will do the work on a subconscious level. But our task is to bring the hidden world of the subconscious up from the depths of our mind into the shining daylight of conscious awareness. Your wide-awake mind needs to pay sustained attention to the subtle impressions your skin will receive sitting in front of the colored light.

So, be curious. Pay attention. Remain in the present, undistracted. When you know which color is being shown, you can prod your attention periodically by mentally telling yourself, "This is red," or "This is blue."

In Stage 3, your self-talk will change. "What color is this? What am I feeling?" Asking these questions will keep you in the present moment.

Feel free to wave your hands near the screen during all three stages, facing your palms toward the color. Also, turn your head slowly from side to side, and nod up and down. In the past, people have remarked the sinuses inside their nostrils were particularly sensitive to light. Also, experiment with opening your mouth, but make sure doing so doesn't allow light to leak through the edges of the blindfold.

You can work with the three stages of the digital color wheel at
**www.learnmindsight.com/preparation.html**

# BRAIN TRAINING

Mind Sight training involves changing the way your brain processes information. Assuming Mind Sight is new to you, it will be helpful to stimulate your brain to grow new connections. Brain training is a way of creating positive stress.

By now, most people are aware the theory of "right brain, left brain" thinking, called "hemispheric dominance," is a myth[50]. According to the hemispheric dominance myth, the right and left sides of the brain are responsible for the following types of processing (OECD, n. d.):

Left Brain                          Right Brain

verbal                              non-verbal, visuo-spatial
sequential                          simultaneous
logical                             holistic
analytical                          integrating
rational/intellectual               intuitive/emotional

Although the brain does not actually isolate these processes into one side or the other, the myth helps us describe personality styles. It's probably why the myth has lasted so long. Even though it's a myth, I still use the phrases "right brain" and "left brain" because they're useful for describing people.

A left-brained person is described as being more interested in facts, logic, and what the five senses perceive. A right-brained person, on the other hand, makes decisions using their gut, feeling their intuition.

In learning Mind Sight, both types of processing are required. I propose a mental model for thinking about the brain with regard to Mind Sight. To be clear, mental models are intended to communicate a helpful idea, *not* to prove how something works.

I propose when someone first exposes themselves to a color, their initial experiences could be described as "right-brained," meaning they use intuition. They're visuo-spatial, and they're immediate. A seer's task then, is to extend that experience into the "left-brain," meaning being able to identify the color and verbally label it, which requires language.

---

[50] OECD. (n. d.). *Neuromyth 6*: The left brain/right brain myth. https://www.oecd.org/education/ceri/neuromyth6.htm

They can perceive subtle impressions (right-brain), and *consciously know them* to be what we call, "the color green" (left-brain). Therefore, in this model, left-side and right-side processes have to work together.

The preparatory practices of dream recollection, the daytime practices, the guided visualizations, and using the digital color wheel naturally train the brain for Mind Sight. To perceive a color and identify it by a certain name, the verbal/logical/linear processes and non-verbal/intuitive/visuo-spatial processes must work together.

As you work from Phase 1 to 14, your brain will continue to improve the way various processes communicate with each other.

Yet, you might consider engaging in other types of brain training to help stimulate new connections. I offer three suggestions here. Based on them, you'll be able to come up with others to achieve the same result. Whatever exercise you choose, it should be *challenging* for you and require *sustained intentional attention*. If it's too easy or if you're not paying enough attention, your brain won't respond with new growth.

Another benefit to these brain exercises is they serve as boredom busters. Taking a break from regular training to do them instead keeps things fresh and fun while still training your brain.

BRAIN EXERCISE #1: Non-dominant hand drawing

If you are right-handed, you'll do this drawing exercise holding a pen or pencil in your left hand. If you're left-handed, then do the opposite. Your subject for this piece of art will be your dominant hand. If you're right-handed, you'll use your left hand to do a "still-life" drawing of your right. Since the right hemisphere moves the left side of the body and vice-versa, you'll be using one side of your brain in a way it's unaccustomed to, forcing it to learn and *grow.*

Take your time with this. You'll outline your wrist to your fingertips. Then draw the nails. Then draw the lines over the knuckles and any other wrinkles, freckles, hairs, or other marks. Then add some shading. Don't be surprised if you end up with a lovely piece of abstract art. Your drawing may be more "artistic" than if you had done it with your dominant hand and the "left-side" processes of your brain.

Suppose you enjoyed the exercise and want to use it again. In that case, you can draw any object in your home, still using your non-dominant hand. You might also experiment with using chalk, charcoal, pastels, or watercolor on different kinds of paper.

BRAIN EXERCISE #2: Crossing the Midline with Juggling

Occupational therapists who work with children are familiar with the term "bilateral coordination." It means being able to use both hands together to complete tasks, such as buttoning a shirt. The concept of "crossing the midline" is important in developing bilateral coordination. On the website, *The Autism Helper*, Katie McKenna writes, "When a child easily crosses the midline, he can use his dominant right hand to reach across to grab an item on the left side of his body without having to stop and switch hands in the middle".[51]

Crossing the midline is important for children. Mind Sight training invites us into a second childhood of sorts. We can stimulate new brain growth by learning a skill that requires crossing the midline. This is why I suggest juggling. Juggling requires hand-eye coordination as well as moving the right hand to catch an object on the left side and vice versa.

An easy and effective way to start is by using juggling scarves and learning to use three of them at the same time. You can buy inexpensive juggling scarves from online stores. You'll find excellent juggling tutorials on YouTube using the search phrase "scarf juggling basics (beginner)."

BRAIN EXERCISE #3: Crossing the Midline with Midbrain Exercises

YouTube is filled with numerous instructional videos for midbrain exercises. Most of them come from India, where "midbrain activation" has become immensely popular as well as controversial. I mention these exercises here not because of some of the extreme claims made about them, but because they fulfill important requirements for stimulating brain growth. They are challenging to learn, and they require sustained intentional attention.

By learning and practicing these midline-crossing movements, you create new opportunities for your brain to grow.

I have found some of the YouTube videos[52] a little too fast to learn from. Therefore, I've created a tutorial video to make it easier for you to learn them.

You can watch my midbrain tutorial at **www.learnmindsight.com/preparation.html**

---

[51] McKenna, Katie. (n. d.). Why Crossing the Midline Matters. *The Autism Helper.* https://theautismhelper.com/why-crossing-the-midline-matters/

[52] Find these YouTube videos by searching with the phrase "midbrain activation brain gym."

# ATTITUDES FOR SUCCESS

Earlier, we discussed two views on learning, the "growth" mindset and the "fixed" mindset. Hopefully, you made the conscious decision to adopt a growth mindset after reading about them. Once you know your options, you have control.

I would also like to suggest attitudes for success more specific to Mind Sight training. Let us ask, "How do I know if I'm succeeding?" The answer will give us a clue about how we should maintain our attitude throughout the training.

The training journals in Part 3 offer an opportunity for you to track your progress. One way to do this is to measure your success mathematically. You could count how many times you were right about a card, and compare that to how many times you were wrong. I did this a lot, only to realize later on that this was an **inherently stressful thing to do** to myself.

So, the first thing I suggest is, don't track how often you're right or wrong. If I could scream this from a rooftop I would, "It's not about being right or wrong!" Doing so is using a fixed mindset. Instead, we should treat this is an adventure, an exploration. Using a growth mindset removes the stress and pressure we might otherwise place on ourselves. When it comes to subtle perception, stress greatly impairs our ability.

Let us return to the question, "How do I know if I'm succeeding?" We can reply to that question with other questions:

- Are you becoming more relaxed during your training?
- Are you having more fun?
- Are you becoming a more relaxed and fun person overall?
- Are you becoming less harsh and judgmental of yourself and others?
- Are you kinder and more forgiving?
- Is your self-confidence increasing?
- Do you care less about what other people think of you?

If you notice yourself turning every session into a test or competition against yourself, you're heading in the wrong direction. Become like children. Be a friend to yourself. Make curiosity and humor your constant companions.

I hope at some point in your training you realize Mind Sight is about far more than seeing without your eyes. It's about being a loving person.

You'll see.

# LEARN FROM MY MISTAKES

I'm happy to share the mistakes I made in the course of my training. I'm sure I'll make more in the future because that's part of continued learning. Regardless, the ones below are important to be aware of. It will serve you well to recognize when you've accidentally fallen into them. I've designed the 14 Phases to avoid these mistakes as much as possible. If you decide to "go rogue," learning about these now will be even more critical and time-saving.

MISTAKE #1 - TESTING WITHOUT LEARNING

This was my biggest mistake. I started teaching myself by *not* teaching myself. Silly, right? I thought I could throw on my blindfold, hold up a randomly selected card, and eventually perceive its color. The problem was, I hadn't *taught* my brain to convert the subtle impressions I'd receive through my skin or consciousness into the appropriate visual representation of the actual color.

Phase 1 is about familiarization and learning. You'll know which two colors you're working with each session. So, when you're holding up a black card, you'll know it's black. Then, when you begin to see something in your mind's eye, or notice a strange mood, or feel a sort of mental texture, your brain will learn, "These experiences mean 'black.'"

To this end, you should consider spending several days or weeks using the Preparatory Exercises before starting Phase 1.

MISTAKE #2 - RECORDING EVERYTHING

Having already written other books on consciousness development, I suspected I might write about seeing without eyes someday. Therefore, I took copious notes after each session. During some sessions, I also used an audio recorder, remarking on my experience and whether I was "right or wrong" after each card. I often recorded myself on video as well.

These behaviors added stress similar to what I might experience had I practiced in front of a live audience. It's too much! I'm still glad I did it because I learned valuable lessons I could share with you here. But if you want to help yourself, don't film or record yourself. But there's an exception.

You could film yourself once in a while after you've noticed an increase in accuracy over time. Watching videos of yourself succeeding will increase your self-confidence. And self-confidence helps us relax.

So, when you record yourself, do it knowing only you (and your partner if you have one) will watch it. If you're fantasizing about making awesome videos to share online afterward, that could be too stressful for certain personalities.


MISTAKE #3 - BEING IMPATIENT

I knew it was possible learning Mind Sight could take months or even years. But deep down inside, I didn't want it to take that long. I knew I should be patient, but I wasn't. Looking back on my journal, I can see that I was improving over time. I also noticed that my improvement wasn't a straight shot. I had good days and bad days. It often felt like I was taking two steps forward then one step back. Sometimes, it was more like one step forward and three steps back.

My journal conclusively showed that when I was frustrated during a session, my ability suffered greatly. Sometimes, that frustration came from expecting too much from myself, too soon.

The book's description says the Mind Sight exercises can last anywhere from 1 to 3 years. I wouldn't be surprised if some readers purchased it thinking to themselves, "It shouldn't take that long. I can do it faster." And maybe you can. I hope you can, that would be great! But if it takes longer, I hope you can be a patient person and surrender your hurry. In time, you will see this is about the journey, not the destination. Younger adults may not understand that yet, but I'm old enough to know it's true.

MISTAKE #4 - BEING TOO STRICT

I tried as much as possible to follow the same routine when first learning Mind Sight. I had a specific chair and table and scheduled the same time every day to practice. The problem was that my schedule had to change some days, and then I didn't practice at all. Later in the day, there was available time, but I wasn't flexible enough to do it then. Or, sometimes, my body was too sore or tired to sit up in my chair for an hour straight, and I felt uncomfortable while training.

After I figured this out, some of my best sessions happened while lying on the couch. Others happened while lying in bed, in the dark, late at night.

So, be flexible. Make yourself comfortable. Alter any aspect of training to make it work better for you.

## MISTAKE #5 - TURNING A SESSION INTO A GUESSING GAME

From Phase 2 onward, your sessions will include opportunities to perceive a card without first knowing what color, letter, or number is on it. Phase 2 assumes you've spent adequate time with the Preparatory Exercises as well as Phase 1.

You should patiently perceive each card before deciding what you think you're holding. Using the glue technique[53], you'll verify your accuracy each time without needing to remove your blindfold.

Sometimes, I would become impatient or frustrated. Instead of slowly receiving impressions, I relied on the first impulse that came to mind and immediately decided what it was, "It's blue!" Upon discovering I was incorrect, I repeated the process, quickly deciding, "It's red!" still *without* actually having perceived anything.

It got worse the more tired I was or the closer I was to finishing the session. In these cases, I'd completely stopped being a patient perceiver and turned this into a guessing game instead. It felt like playing roulette. Red or black. "It's gotta be black!" Nope, wrong guess.

So, if ever you find yourself guessing, it's time to stop. Realize that you're no longer exercising the appropriate neural networks, and you're wasting your time. It might be a good time to take a day or two off from training and check your motivation.

## MISTAKE #6 - USING EXTREME LIGHTING

In the beginning, I spent many sessions beneath an extremely bright fluorescent lamp. It was the kind used by photographers and filmmakers. I thought a brighter light reflecting off the cards would help my perception. Eventually I realized the focused intensity of the light worked against me, as if the white glare wiped out the "color quality" of each card. In time, I realized the balanced ambient light in a room was sufficient. Also, casual, deeply relaxed sessions in pitch blackness reclining in my bedroom at night proved that light wasn't necessary at all. I enjoyed the added benefit of not worrying about light leaking into the blindfold.

Therefore, I recommend using natural light, or typical indoor lighting, and also experimenting in the dark.

---

[53] This technique is discussed in Part 3.

# NOTES FROM THE FIELD

It can be difficult to experience something for the first time when you have no idea what to expect. We learn by forming relationships between previous events in our lives. Using our past experiences, we create expectations about the future.

Yet, Mind Sight is a massive leap from anything we know. Most of us[54] have used our eyes, ears, nose, tongue, and skin all our lives, and we take them for granted. We've never had to rely on the darkness behind our closed eyelids to inform us about our surroundings.

Therefore, a natural first question as you begin your training might simply be, "What's it like?"

I have to be careful here, because I'm aware that a person's *expectation* of an experience has an enormous effect on their *actual* experience.[55] I believe each person practicing Mind Sight will have a unique journey. If I say too much, I'll condition your experience. You may subconsciously be looking to me as this book's author to tell you "what it's supposed to be like." I don't want to do that.

You can empower yourself this very moment by welcoming whatever comes, even if it doesn't match anything I've said, or anything you've heard from other people.

Still, you need *something*. The education sector understands the word "scaffolding" to mean offering someone a tool or structure to help them learn.[56] I also like the commonly known definition of scaffolding as "a temporary structure."

Please forgive me, this is a long way of telling you I'm still going to help you get started by sharing selected notes from my journal. My description of my first perceptions will *help you spot them when they happen to you*. I'll help you begin, but you'll need to go the rest of the way on your own.

---

[54] With consideration of those with congenital or acquired impairments.

[55] Ariely, Dan. (2009). *Predictably Irrational: The Hidden Forces That Shape Our Decisions* (Revised Edition). Harper.

[56] Alber, Rebecca. (2014, January 24). 6 Scaffolding Strategies to Use with Your Students. *Edutopia*. https://www.edutopia.org/blog/scaffolding-lessons-six-strategies-rebecca-alber

My notes also offer a peek into my psychology during my sessions. I don't need to say anything more now. It'll be obvious when you read about the sessions below.

Also, consider what I share as temporary scaffolding. If your journey appears different from mine, it's time to let go of what I've shared. It was never meant to last forever.

My notes below will be headed by a session number. This way, you'll get a sense for how many sessions it took me to gain these first experiences. This is meant to encourage and inspire you. I was a slow learner largely because of the mistakes I discussed in the previous chapter. My process was slow also because I did it alone. If you adjust this training to work with a partner or a group, I'm sure your results may come sooner. But don't rush. Remember my mistake of rushing.

Please read my journal entries carefully. Many of them include valuable kernels that will help you after you've begun training.

Before reading them, you should understand I used a process slightly different from what is being taught in this book. Again, this is based on correcting my own mistakes. But in general, I would work with two or more colors, shuffling multiple cards of each in a big bag, and then pull them out one by one. I was blindfolded the whole time.

For example, if I was working with red and yellow cards, I would drop a card I believed to be red on the floor to my left. If I thought it was yellow, I'd drop it to my right. After my time was up or I'd gone through all the cards in my bag, I'd remove my blindfold and see the results. Were all the cards to my left red? Were all the cards to my right yellow? If not, were they mostly in their correct piles? Or 50/50? Or worse?

I'll make comments about my journal entries when clarification is helpful.

Note: Some notes were transcriptions of what I captured on my audio recorder or video camera. Others were written down immediately following a session.

## Session 2

"I want it to be red, but I think that wanting is just my imagination because the brightness makes me think this is yellow." - I put it on the yellow side, which was correct.

*Note my emotional bias, wanting it to be red. Guard against your bias.*

**Session 6**

"I noticed myself being unhappy when I was wrong and happy when I was right, and that didn't feel good to me. I realized I didn't want to punish myself emotionally every time I missed. I realized I needed to change my attitude and spent the rest of the time simply asking myself "What color is it?" without trying to pin down an answer..."

**Session 7 with Cierra**

"Meanwhile, Cierra tried her own way, feeling the vibration with her hands with one large yellow page and one large red page, in her office. Then she came to the living room and asked me to randomly put one of the small cards in her hands. She got several correct, in a row.

She was quickly raising and lowering one hand over the card without touching it, while holding it in her other hand. Just going by the feeling, she could discern one color from another. I asked what she'd done in her office beforehand. She said she just stared at the red page while mentally reminding herself 'this is red,' then closing her eyes and *feeling* over the paper with her hand, then doing the same with the yellow. This was her first time doing this."

**Session 8**

"This afternoon, I lied on the couch after lunch and just worked with one small card I grabbed from the pile without seeing what color it was, trying to see it with my blindfold on. I only worked on it for ten or so minutes as I became more relaxed and sleepy, then set it down to take a nap. I peeked to see what color it was, and it was red, which I had suspected."

*Note: This was a brief example of being flexible and casual once in a while.*

**Session 9**

"...I felt like I was actually getting closer, and that's when I got really sleepy suddenly and felt like stopping for the night. I wonder if some part of me is actually afraid of succeeding, or really lazy and knows I can do it but just doesn't want to go "all in" on this... Whatever it is that might be resistant to doing this might actually be holding me back."

**Session 11**

"For the first time I saw a fuzzy dark red patch appear and disappear very quickly. Checking the card, I saw it was red. I felt a subtle level of elation, followed by tiredness and temptation to stop. I kept going for 5-10 more minutes then stopped. Once, what appeared as a pinhole opened up, I thought it looked yellow, but a split second later I had doubts and thought it was just a leak near my nose, and then I thought I saw a streak of red on the lower half of my vision. I checked the card and was surprised to see that it was indeed yellow. Had my mind created the red streak after I felt doubt about the validity of the yellow pinhole?

After that, I decided whenever I saw a pinhole, I would trust it up to the point when I checked the card's color. Feeling any kind of distrust during the process might be problematic, and I figure once I see the card I'll know whether that pinhole was a leak or not. I think I'm doing a little better…"

Note: The phenomenon can occur in different ways. Patches of color might appear, or in this case, a tiny pinprick of light might show up. In either case, distrusting your impression can set you back and even prevent new arisings.

**Session 11 continued**
"A basic point to remember: I need to keep the intention to "look at" (focus on) the card instead of daydreaming while waving the card around (and hoping for something to happen that way)."

**Session 13**
"For this one a little blue dot showed up early on. It also seems brighter under the right side of my eye. I move it up and down the front of my body, and I can sense the movement in front of my heart center. Also, waving in front of the right side it seemed brighter but on the left side it seemed more energetic. I just checked it and it's yellow. That was the first card.

Right away with the second card, holding it in front of my eyes I can sense the energy of it, but I don't know what color it is. I feel in front of my right eye, there's a glow in it or around it (my eye), and it's there even when I'm not holding the card in front of it. Maybe it's just opening up or something.

The second one was yellow. This time I didn't feel anything at the heart chakra, but I did closer to my throat and face.

I can tell I'm tense. I'm short on breath, or not breathing right, so I'm just pausing to relax. I think I'm trying too hard.

On this next one I'm going to take a chance because just one minute into it, I'm waving it near my left temple and it's not "orangish", it's a little brighter than that, so I'm going to guess yellow, we'll see. And…it was yellow.

I'm feeling worn down again, looking at the next card. I'm going to pause and take a few deep breaths, and remind myself to breathe normally (instead of holding my breath) and relax.

On this card, I've been working at it a while, and if I wave it around the left side and the right side of my head, towards the back, there's more of a brightness than anything else, not "orangy." I think it's yellow, we'll see. And it was yellow.

I just noticed something interesting. As I brush the card up and down my arms, for a few seconds, it's like the ambient light around my vision got turned up, it got brighter in general.

On this one, I felt overwhelmed. I wasn't sure if my mind was doing what I wanted it to do. So, I repeated something I've been doing lately, where I wave my hands in front of my face. When I get a sense that I can see my fingers waving in space, I put my finger on the card to direct my attention to the card and help me focus more. And this time when I did that, I moved my hand off the card to the right, and I felt an intensity there on the right, off the card. I moved the card to where my hand had been (to the right) and kept moving it toward the right front corner of my head, near my temple. It seemed to have a darkness to it. Then I moved it to the left side, and I can feel the card off my left front corner, but it's kind of dark, so I think it's red. I'm going to look now, and it is red!

I feel tired right away after getting that one right. Excited, but tired. Tempted to quit. I'm not sure how to relate to that temptation, so I'm going to just rest for a few moments, then try again.

On this next card, when I was waving it in front of my right front corner, it was a little bit dark, but a little bit of brightness in front of the eye. Then I felt compelled to pull it over to my left side. And as I brought it in front of the left front corner, suddenly everything got brighter there. And I want to say brighter on the yellow side, but I'm not sure. It's just more of a general brightness, but it's pretty vivid. So, I'm going to think it's yellow, I'm going to peek now, and it's red.

The thing is, after getting that one wrong, I feel relaxed. I don't get the same response as when I've been correct today. Maybe I'm more at ease with being wrong than with being right. That would be an important psychological issue to consider.

I just started working on this one for a minute, and just holding it in front of my face, and the right side of my temple lit up with a glow. I moved the card to where the glow is happening, and it just seems dark, to have a shadow, and then the glow faded out as I pulled the card back over to the center. I just brushed it over my arms again, but this time, my mind did not start glowing brighter. The alarm already went off, it just seems dark, so I'm going to guess red. And it was yellow."

## Session 14

"Finished the first card of the day. When I started the session I took 10 deep belly breaths to settle in. When I held the card up to my face, a very faint, fuzzy dot showed up in front of my left eye. I tried to look at it with my attention and it faded out just a few seconds later. Then I moved the card around as usual. It seemed brighter under the right side of my jaw. When I moved it over to the right side of my head, there was another faint dot. I can't say it was yellow, but bright, maybe slightly yellowish. Then I moved the card behind my neck and over the top of my head and when I touched the crown of my head, another dot arose in my vision, and I started to think that maybe the card was yellow. I just checked the card and it was yellow.

The second card was difficult because it wasn't giving me much, but toward the end as I waved it in front of my right eye, it was a dark shadow but it had energy to it. Same thing on the left side of my head, as I moved it over, it was like a shadow or an eclipse in that area. So I started to think it was red, and I just checked, and it was red.

This next card is developing a lot of brightness, especially over my left collarbone. It's bright, I'm not quite sure if it's red or yellow. But because it is so bright I'm going to think it's yellow. Let's check. It's red.

On this next one I got a vague blue flash just over the bridge of my nose. This last card is being difficult. I think it's because I'm feeling pressure to stop and go to work, the time pressure. But because of the blue flash, and I am picking up some brightness as I hold it in front of my belly, I get some brightness. I think it's yellow. And it is yellow. That's a good place to stop - on a success."

## Session 15

"Yesterday I realized the importance of telling the difference between seeing what's actually occurring versus seeing what I "think" I'm looking at. In a fraction of a second, my mind starts to imagine (guess) what I'm holding, often right after I receive an actual impression of some sort. If I guess that I'm seeing yellow, then my mind will produce the color yellow *as a memory* and I'll just focus on that instead of keeping my mind directed to the real impressions I'm receiving.

Then my mind gets *stuck* on that guess, and experiences it as if that was what I was actually perceiving. So, I have two experiences that I need to discern going forward - "actual" experience and "make-believe" experience. They're both experiences occurring in the darkness of my awareness, so in a way, they are both a version of my "reality." But I need to have fidelity to "actuality" (what I'm actually experiencing) and not be distracted or taken away by "make-believe" (what I *think* I'm experiencing)."

### Session 17
"Once, I got a distinct yellow flash, in the shape of a horizontal band of light along the lower right side of my face. That card was indeed yellow.

I realized that I have no way of predicting when my mind will be successful, and my attitude is formed without any real basis. I can become pessimistic or optimistic and stay with that line of thinking and feeling, but it's pretty much entirely my choice. The risk of a pessimistic attitude is that it can convince me to end the session sooner, or quit the project entirely. An optimistic attitude will help me maintain my commitment, and make the whole process a lot more enjoyable."

### Session 18
"As soon as I picked up the first card, there was a glimmer over the bridge of my nose. Instead of adjusting my blindfold, I decided to look at it and see what would happen. It faded away on its own. As I wave the card to the left and right of my skull, it looks like a shadow, but there's a glimmer that appears after watching the shadow. The glimmer shows up in front of my face. I can't tell if this is red or yellow.

Still on the first card, it's been a few minutes now. I'm getting a lot of brightness, but I think I'm getting some very dark rusty color on the left side of my head. I think it's red and... it is red.

I'm quietly building up the excitement of having gotten that one correctly. And I'm just saying "Yes! Yes! Yes!" inside of my mind and a sense of celebration, trying to train my mind away from being negative or working against myself.

Second card, a couple minutes into it, it feels like the right side of my head is intensifying. I don't want to say it's filling with energy, but it's intensifying because there's a light quality to it, and it's almost like it's blinding, although it really isn't about being blinded by bright lights. Perhaps something is happening inside my head. And I know from the past this intensity doesn't necessarily mean it's a yellow card, even though there's a brightness to it. I'm going to be patient before finishing this card."

*Note: The last paragraph addressed a strange phenomenon that occurs periodically. A very bright, white light will enter one side of my head, eventually filling my entire vision. It makes it impossible to perceive the card, and I simply have to wait for it to fade on its own. I could guess what it is, but that wouldn't be helpful without good evidence.*

**Session 18 continued**
"This card, as I wave it to the right of my chest, of my heart, and I can see the movement. I just got a spark of red show up as I was saying that! It appeared as if it was in front of only my right eye. The front right of my head is intensifying as I bring the card there. To my open mouth, there's a slight bit of brightness that comes in. The card was red.

The next card is making the right side of my head intense again, it's almost blinding. It's not having the same effect as before from holding it to my open mouth. In front of my chest and to the left, it's like a little glow follows along when I wave the card up and down, the glow rises and falls at the chest level. The card is red.

Next card, I'm getting a brightness behind my left ear. [The timer marking one hour goes off, and I feel rushed to finish] Waving it even further back behind the left side of my head. There's a lightness there, but it's not so sharp. It's muted, and I wanted to describe it as "creamy." I'm going to look now....it's yellow."

**Session 19**
"Precondition: I felt nervous because I'd taken two days off, and wondered if this would hinder me. Had whatever changes to my mind/brain that I'd cultivated from the start gone away? Or would taking a break end up being helpful? I also haven't done yoga in three days, but I feel very mentally relaxed this afternoon, now that I have a break from school.

This afternoon's session lasted around 90 minutes. I had set a timer, but accidentally turned it off when getting up after the 60 minute bell to rest on the couch for a few minutes. Keeping my blindfold on during my break, I was reaching around to avoid hitting furniture and accidentally touched my phone's screen and turned off the timer.

At the end of the session, I removed my blindfold and was happy to see the cards on the floor on either side of me. To my left, I'd dropped all the cards I thought were red. Looking at the pile, I saw 5 red cards and only 1 yellow! To my right, I'd dropped all the cards I thought were yellow. I ended up with 7 yellow cards and only 1 red! That means of 14 cards, only 2 were incorrect. 86% correct. This is the first major success I've had."

*Note: In this and other entries, you'll notice I'm scoring myself with a "percentage correct." Scoring myself this way added too much stress in the long run. I don't recommend doing it.*

"If my estimated session time of 90 minutes is correct, that means I spent, on average, 6.4 minutes on each card, which is faster than before.

I just noticed something that I probably have experienced all along. There's a distinctly different sensation in my head, physically, that differs from when I'm "sort of" paying attention and "sort of" being present, and when I'm on point. When I'm on point, it feels more pressurized in my head. It's not painful, it's not intense, it's just like there's a shift, like there's more of *something* happening in my head."

Photo of my training area taken after Session 19

**Session 20**

"Tonight I did my session right before bed. I was tired, and my session only lasted 35 minutes. However, I looked at my piles at the end and saw in the yellow pile I had 5 yellow cards and 1 red card. In the red pile, I had 5 red cards and 1 yellow card. 83% correct.

I averaged 3 minutes per card, which is much faster than usual. There were a few times when I just felt right away that the card was one color or the other. Overall, I'd say most of my *knowing* the color of the card comes from how my head feels as I move the card around it. It's about sensation at this point, not actual color. But still, there have been a few times when the luminosity of the card, whether it's a general glow of a very subtle shade, or a quick flash, has successfully indicated which card it was.

At this point, I make sure to take ten belly breaths in between cards. If I get distracted or unfocused while working with a card, I take a break and breathe deeply for a few moments, then refocus my attention. Before I reach for a new card, I set a mental intention of "Here. Now." as a way to point my mind to the card.

I think the two times I was incorrect were from deciding too fast and from once again not trusting what I was actually seeing and following what I wanted the card to be."

**Session 23**

"At least one mistake occurred when I wasn't totally focused on seeing the card. I remember that my mind was distracted and wondering if it was time to start using cards of other colors, like blue. Then I realized that *just the act of thinking about other colors* during this exercise was going to work against me, since that takes me away from "actuality."

I just correctly identified a yellow card. I want to note the reason I chose yellow was because a certain brightness was showing up behind my *right* ear. But until now, yellow has been showing up more by my *left* ear. So, it seems that the space behind my left ear is beginning to open up (in its ability to perceive)."

**Session 24**

"On this card, a couple of minutes in, I got a very brief point of red, like a smudge of red, and I didn't trust it, so I kept working with the card longer.

And then I saw some brightness, which made me think "Aha! It's yellow!" But I kept working with it longer, and then my head started to feel physically different, and then I decided it was red based on the new impressions (after my head felt physically different). And it was indeed red."

**Session 25**

"I did a brief session this afternoon, only 25 minutes. I did really badly. On the red side, I had 2 yellow cards and 1 red. On the yellow side, I had 6 red cards and 1 yellow. Success rate was only 20%. That's not only "chance," but significantly *below* chance. In parapsychology, this is called "psi missing." It means that psychic ability *was* involved, but it was making me choose the wrong colors *really well*, instead of the correct colors."

**Session 28**

"I think of the roulette table, and how some people will bet on black when they see that black has come up six times in a row. They see a trend which does not exist, since each spin is unique. Another gambler might say, "Black has come up so many times in a row, *this time it must* be red!" which is another version of bias. When I happen to select two red cards in a row, some part of me wants the next card to be yellow, and this is a problem.

On this card, I was experimenting with extending my consciousness out beyond my body to see if I could connect with the card better, and then I heard a loud bang come from the kitchen. I took off the blindfold to see what it was. Cierra's water bottle, which was on the kitchen counter, had fallen over. I have no way of knowing if I did that somehow, or if something else caused it. But I note it here in case other anomalies occur in the future.

*Note: Yes, sometimes strange, unexpected things happen when you open your awareness.*

**Session 29**

"(After having a really good session). I don't understand how I did so well when I never had a glimpse of an actual color. All of my decisions were based on how my head physically responded when the cards were held close to it at different angles, and on the amount of glow they produced. There was also something else, another kind of "knowing" which I don't know how to describe right now. I don't think it's the same thing as "intuition" as most people define that word. It might be more like how a goldfish experiences its world, fully reactive in the present moment without overthinking. I suppose this is where a person would have to experience it themselves to know what I'm talking about."

**Session 30**

"Blue seems to have a foggy lightness to it. However, near the end of the session, my perceptual field grew dark suddenly, as if a shadow had fallen over everything. I don't know if this meant my mind was acclimating to the color, or if it just "turned off." Naturally, time will tell."

*Note: This phenomenon is the opposite of the one from session 18 with the bright light filling my head. In this session, it was as if a darkness overcame my whole perceptual field like an eclipse.*

**Session 35**

"In general, I could identify the blue cards by the brightness that would happen under my chin and under the right side of my jaw. Sometimes I could pick up on the foggy haze when I held them in front of my face.

I identified the red cards mostly by the headache I'd get in the front right corner of my head when I held them close. There were a few times I mistook them for blue cards because of their brightness, but overall red is a darker color than blue.

I kept trying just like before. If I thought a card was red, I dropped it to my left side. If I thought it was blue, I'd drop it on my right. This way I could count how many times I was correct. On the blue side, I ended up with 9 blue and 5 red. On the red side, I ended up with 7 red and only 3 blue.

With 14 cards on the blue side and 10 on the red, I think I was psychologically biased toward blue, probably because it's a new color, and because I "like" it better than red because I seem to pick it up easier. But that bias made me more apt to mistake red for blue.

Since I had only 3 blue in the red pile, and 7 red, I think that's a good sign that I'm doing a better job distinguishing colors than I've done in the past. I feel happy after this session."

**Session 36 - A series of comments I recorded after each card in this session. I was working with red and blue.**

"This is the very first card. I'm not getting a lot from it, but I don't feel any pressure in the right side of my head. And, there is a slight bit of shine when I hold it under my chin. So, I think it's blue. [correct].

Second card. On the left side of my head, it appeared like a dark shadow. On the right side, it was also dark, but I definitely got some pressure in my head. So, I think it's red. [correct]

This is the third card. It's a lot more difficult now. There's not as much brightness. I'm not getting any pressure on the right side of my head. But I think there's enough brightness in general for me to call it blue. [correct]

Again, no headache on the right side, and definitely some brightness, especially below the chin. [blue] And if I didn't say it, I thought that one was blue. [so this was correct]

As soon as I brought it up to my left side, it was again like a dark shadow coming over. And it was dark as I brought it over the right side of my head. So, I think it's red. [correct]

This next one is just generally lighter, there's no shadow with it. And now I'm starting to see the movement of the card in front of my face a little bit more, the same way I can sometimes see my fingers and hands in front of my face. I see the card a little bit like that. Not with any color, but with the sense of "fog" moving. I think this is blue. [incorrect]

This one I also think it's blue, it's just got a lighter sense to it in my mind, and I noticed, this time around, behind my left ear, I see the brightness there, and it's also got a gray quality, almost a blue quality, but more gray, so I think this one's blue. [incorrect]

That last one threw me off, I was so sure it was blue, but it was red. On this one, I'm getting brightness under my chin, my jaw. But I don't feel confident calling it blue. I want to say that the fog around it is more of a rust color. So now I'm just confused. I can see the movement. I just think it's blue. [incorrect]"

### Session 38

"This is so much more enjoyable since I'm not tracking whether I'm right or wrong during this session. I can take my time with a card. It's a different attitude, and I think it's a different way of the brain working. I have a sense that I'm doing a little better than last night, but it doesn't matter. There were even a couple times when I allowed myself to say "I don't know." It felt good giving myself permission to do that."

### Session 48

"… there were three times during the session when I chose a red card because I actually perceived the *color* red in some way. Either it was a brief smudge or splotch of red on my mental field, or a background radiance of red."

### Session 49

"I did something several times which I believe helped me to be more accurate. After working with a card for a while, I would sometimes sense when my conscious mind was coming to conclusions too soon, or was being biased, largely in response to whatever the previous color was. So, I'd put the card down for a half a minute or so, and just relax and let go. Then, I'd raise the card up again and continue the process of looking. Often, my thoughts about the color were different than they were before I took that brief "break."

Another thing I did differently was to use a "qigong" style of looking. I was reading a qigong book this evening before the session, and one section discussed how to use one's eyes during qigong. Essentially, the instructions were to look *without* looking, and to look "inside" at the same time as looking out. This is a relaxed, non-focused, non-grasping style of perceiving. I thought it would be interesting to try it tonight, instead of looking as intently as I usually do toward the card.

### Session 53

"I decided to shift gears and work with black and white cards. I had cut them up into small squares back at the very beginning, when I cut up the other colors. But this was my first time working with them. I didn't have large cards for them, so to acclimate my mind to each color, I first worked with the stack of white cards, spending a couple of minutes with each until I received some type of input. After about 20 minutes, I did the same thing with the stack of black cards.

In the darkness, the white card came through as a very faint and creamy sort of impression. The dark card gave me even less information. Still, they seemed distinct from each other.

Then, I shuffled the two stacks (while blindfolded), threw them into the bag, shook it up, and began drawing them out one by one. When I was finished with the whole bag, I took my blindfold off to see that on the black pile, I had 17 black cards and only 1 white. On the white pile, it was the reverse, with 17 white and only 1 black.

This was my best result ever! But I couldn't really celebrate. I wasn't surprised that I did that well, actually. The thing is, I could tell the paper texture for the black cards was smoother and heavier than the white cards. I'd been careful to buy the same type of card stock, but still, these felt different from each other.

Because of that, I can't even be sure at this point if I actually perceived visual differences between black and white. I wonder if it's possible that my mind produced the impressions based on the tactile sensation of the card. I have no doubt it could do it quickly enough for me to believe I was honestly perceiving them visually.

The only way to be sure is to work with the cards again, but in a way that allows me to lift them up without touching the cards themselves. I'm thinking about gluing a popsicle stick to each one so I can lift them up without touching them. Until then, I'll move back to the other colors."

**Session 59**
"I noticed that it was often helpful to stop, put the card down, and take some deep breaths and let go for a few seconds before holding it up again. I realized I'd gotten out of the habit of taking several breaths in between cards. It's important to give myself a break between cards as well as when working on any individual card, otherwise it's like trying to exercise this new function non-stop, which could be exhausting to my brain."

**Session 60**
"After putting on my blindfold, I started with the large red card, with the intention of conditioning my mind to know this card as "red." A few moments into the exercise, I moved the card so it was just several inches away from the space between my left cheekbone and ear, at the height of my ear and up the side of my head.

Suddenly, I noticed a very faint, warm, rusty hue. It was like an aura, meaning that it wasn't a solid color, but it appeared "off the edge" of the space between my cheekbone and ear. It was the furthest "edge" to the left. It felt like it was just past the curve of my head, to the back. Noticing this hue, I kept the card in that region, gently and slowly moving it around while trying to take in as much of that experience as possible, as if to memorize it. If I focused too much on it, it seemed to dissipate. But as long as I remained relaxed, I could perceive this hue, subtle as it was.

I tried doing the same on the right side of my head, but the hue didn't appear there.

Then I did the same exercise with the large green card. No hue appeared for it, although its general "glow" was brighter than that of the red card. I also thought I noticed a dark, mossy green shade to the blackness of my overall visual field."

**Other notes from this session:**
"It was more obvious than ever how much my mind creates its own experience by covering over what is actually happening. There were instances when immediately after reaching for a new card, or after touching one, or even the moment after lifting it in front of my head, when my mind tried to guess the color instead of waiting to see whatever was actually there in front of it. It couldn't handle the darkness. It couldn't handle the not-knowing. It immediately filled that gap with its own version of reality.

I've been meditating for years, and this idea of a mind unwilling to be present is very familiar. The same thing goes for the idea about a mind uncomfortable with "the unknown."

I'm also aware of the psychological concept of heuristics. The mind converts moments of life into *heuristics*, shortcuts which allow it to process information and make decisions as quickly as possible. As long as most of the heuristics are correct, we can get along in the world quite successfully. Most importantly, heuristics allow us to identify dangerous situations quickly and respond by running away, either physically, mentally, or emotionally...

... Some part of my mind feels compelled to replace the darkness, the non-knowing, with a color, any color, in order to feel safe and secure. In my case, whether the color is right or wrong doesn't affect my survival. And whether it's right or wrong, it makes that part of my mind feel safe.

I hope the fact this mental function is becoming more obvious is a sign that the *other* part of my mind, the part that can remain in the present and accept the darkness, is getting stronger. I think that's the part which is learning how to see without eyes."

## Session 66

"What stood out today were the few times I realized I was arguing with myself before deciding what color I thought I was holding. It was like a script in my head, "I think it's x color, but I'm not really sure, it's probably the other color, but I'm going to say it's this color anyway." And every time I ran that script in my head and chose a color, I was wrong.

It's as if I know what the correct color is already, and yet the dominant part of my personality refuses to choose it for some strange reason. The kicker is that I watch it happening inside of me, and I know what's happening, and *still* I choose the wrong color. I have some strange trust issues with myself, it seems, and I think it's rooted in the fear of being wrong."

## Session 82

"[white and black] affected my mind in a way opposite to what I expected. The white card didn't provoke much of an effect at all, almost as if it wasn't there, so I thought it would've been the black card. When I held up the black card (without knowing it was black), I was surprised to get a sense of gold from it, slightly different than yellow. It was just a brief flash, but I caught it…"

## Session 86

"Up to now, I've completely shut out the creative side of my mind for this process. I've been afraid that I'd end up making up colors which weren't really there. But today, I allowed the creativity in. Not a lot, just a crack. As if I opened up a door to my creative side just a tiny little bit, allowing only a sliver of light from that other room to penetrate the darkness I've been keeping myself in.

I'm not sure exactly how I allowed (or provoked) the creative function to get involved. It was mostly a matter of giving myself permission, while keeping myself from imagining anything and everything that could possibly enter my mind. I kept to a single question, "If I *imagined* the card which was actually in front of my head right now, how would it appear?"

I used the word "imagined." But after asking myself that question and returning my attention to the actual card, I refrained from actively imagining anything. Instead, it was like gently "taking my foot off the brake" of my imagination, so to speak, and allowing it to influence my experience *ever so slightly*. I allowed it to *color* my experience.

I got the next couple of cards right, and became very excited. I stopped at that point, as I needed to leave for work. I was also afraid of getting the next card wrong. I was so happy to get a couple of cards right after allowing another part of myself to participate, and I wanted to savor that success for a little while, knowing future sessions might not go as well.

I'm keenly aware this may have been a fluke, but after months of making almost no progress, I needed to give this to myself, if only for one day.

**Session 92**
"I decided to do more training, so I picked up the cards again and shuffled them after putting my blindfold back on. But instead of sitting up on the couch, I decided to stay reclined since I was still a little sleepy. I thought I'd allow myself to be very casual and relaxed with the process.

It only took one round to see that something had changed. I had gotten a few cards correctly. The same thing happened with another round. Then, I did another round, in which I got six out of seven cards correct. I was wrong about the yellow card, because I thought it was black. I often confuse yellow and black because black gives off a richness to it, something akin to yellow or gold, but effervescent, not solid. It's something else which I don't know how to describe."

# PART 2

## ACROSS SPACE AND TIME

# Remote Viewers, Meet the Seers
# Seers, Meet the Remote Viewers

Remote viewing (RV) and Mind Sight are two sides of the same coin. They both involve perception by means which defy ordinary explanation. They are both abilities accessible by most people and which can be improved with regular practice.[57]

In this chapter, I'd like to highlight aspects of both disciplines that can help remote viewers and seers develop. I also hope to encourage the cross-pollination of ideas.

At the very least, seers may benefit by including remote viewing as a type of cross training or boredom-busting in their regimen.

Some readers may be familiar with remote viewing from watching the 2020 film "Superhuman: The Invisible Made Visible."[58] For a much more thorough introduction to the concept and history of RV, I highly recommend the 2019 movie "Third Eye Spies."[59]

What sets RV apart from plain clairvoyance is the use of a specific protocol. Here is a basic example:

1. The remote viewer does their session at a specific, designated time

2. They are given a coordinate or a "target reference number" which represents the target they are attempting to perceive. This acts as a focal point and prevents the mind from engaging in guessing.

3. They record their impressions on a transcript (if written) or recording device (if spoken).

4. They are shown the actual target at some point in the future to verify the accuracy of their impressions. This is called "feedback."

---

[57] You can learn and practice remote viewing with groups like the Applied Precognition Project (APP) at www.AppliedPrecog.com and the International Remote Viewing Association (IRVA) at www.IRVA.org

[58] Cory, Caroline. (Director). (2020). *Superhuman: The Invisible Made Visible*. Omnium Media.

[59] Mungia, Lance. (Director). (2019). *Third Eye Spies*. Conscious Universe Films.

For example, here is a transcript of a remote viewing session I did[60]. I was attempting to perceive a picture my wife Cierra would show me the following day. I drew my perceptions on a blank sheet.

Notice the wing shape in the upper right-hand corner. Inside it, I wrote my felt impressions, "White. Like a wing? Up high." I added more impressions in the lower center of the page, "Up, rising up. Animal-feel. Yellow [illegible], like pineapple."

There is another shape in the bottom left corner, which is long and pointed. Then the final shape on the bottom has another impression written inside of it, "metallic." The center of the page shows what could be a birthday cake and some round object with windows or holes.

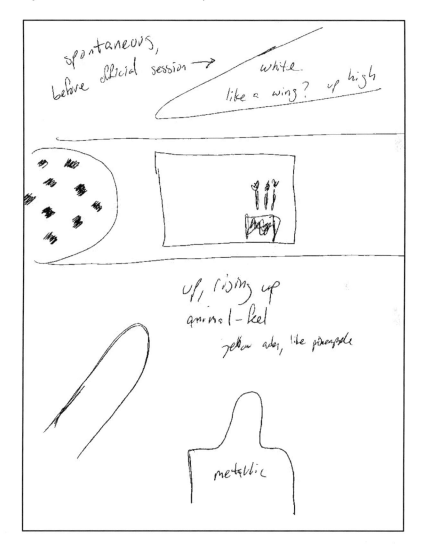

---

[60] An in-depth explanation of this and other sessions can be found inside *Signal and Noise*, which also serves as training manual with numerous exercises.

Now, let's take a look at the actual photo she sent me the next day.

We can see that my session had "hits" as well as "misses." The notion of "wing" and "metallic" and the sense of "Up, rising up" are accurate. The long, pointed drawing resembles the plane's fuselage.

But what about "Yellow… like a pineapple," "animal-feel," and the birthday cake?

Discrepancies like these are common in remote viewing, at least for beginners, because the mind is filled with endless thoughts, memories, and associations continually churning in and out of conscious awareness. Part of a remote viewer's challenge is to improve their ability to identify high-quality impressions from the target, called "signal," and fewer random thoughts, called "noise."

Mind Sight is more direct and precise. For the vast majority of training, the target is a color, shape, letter, or number. As a seer's vision opens up, they can see pictures and even the whole environment in real-time as if their eyes are open. But for this chapter, let's focus on the concept of training to see a specific color.

A remote viewer could benefit from training in Mind Sight to enhance their ability to perceive colors accurately. Perhaps in my example above, I would have picked up on the gray color of the aircraft or the blue sky. And, I wouldn't have perceived yellow if my accuracy was better.

Mind Sight is different from basic clairvoyance similarly to RV:

1. The seer begins their session at a specific time.

2. No coordinate is used. Rather, the target is held close by.

3. The seer verbally states their impressions.

4. Just like a remote viewing session's "feedback," seers see their target afterward to verify their accuracy.

For both seers and remote viewers, feedback adds value to the learning process. By comparing one's impressions to the actual target, seers and remote viewers become more adept at discerning the impressions that arise in their minds and learning how their minds work.

Training in Mind Sight may be beneficial if a remote viewer wants to improve their accuracy perceiving colors or contrasting shadows (black and white). Also, some remote viewers believe that seeing letters and numbers is extremely difficult, if not impossible. Mind Sight can do a lot to change that belief.

Suppose a seer wants to expand their ability to perceive complex scenery rather than simple colors or shapes. In that case, training in Remote Viewing may likewise be beneficial.

If, whether by gradual development or a spontaneous opening, a person can perceive an entire scene as if they were standing there, that would be a profound achievement.

At this point, we could suggest that any person generally interested in psychic perception would do well to cross-train with both modalities. This will lead to skill-building and more opportunities for fun.

I have personal reasons for appreciating feedback. Many years ago, I consulted a "psychic" about my girlfriend's missing cat, Juniper. He told me he "saw" the scene of a coyote snapping up Juniper and that she was dead. With that, we finally mourned her loss.

When these types of psychics make life predictions or give advice, they rarely expect any feedback. We were quite surprised when Juniper showed up at our door a couple of months later, having survived the cold winter. A little while later, another psychic told me my father would be dead within months. But he's still here with us today and doing just fine.

Feedback ensures integrity. Lack of feedback can cause harm.

# PRECOGNITION & RETROCOGNITION

Practicing precognition, retrocognition, telepathy, and long-distance perception[61] are included here for two reasons.

First, they serve the same purpose that predicting the lottery did for my remote viewing friends. They add an element of fun, novelty, and curiosity to your training.

Second, successful experiments in these abilities help answer the question, "Is Mind Sight a physical phenomenon (of the body), or is it a non-physical phenomenon (of consciousness)?"

Perhaps when the color or letter is held in front of one's face, the skin can perceive it and let the brain know what's being shown. In this case, the term "dermo-optical perception" is applicable (dermo -> dermis = skin).

Yet what about perceiving a color or letter that won't be shown until the future? Or which is placed in a different room, or inside a box, "out of sight" from one's skin? In that case, the mind uses more subtle means to obtain the information. It transcends time and space.

The exercises below are intended as boredom busters. And you can also dedicate extra time to them to improve your psychic ability.

Start simple! Suppose you're working on Phase 1 exercises. In that case, you'll know that each session only focuses on two colors and that you will already know what those two colors are.

For example, you may decide to practice precognition on a particular day using only red and blue cards. You'll take your stacks of 10 red and blue cards and shuffle them up. Then, you'll randomly select a card, which you'll look *at in the future*.

Once you're working on Phase 3, you can shuffle and choose between three colors, and in Phase 4, all five colors. This isn't "cheating" or making it "too easy." It's *skillfully training yourself one step at a time* to build your self-confidence as you go.

---

[61] Telepathy and long-distance perception are discussed in the next chapter.

# PRACTICING PRECOGNITION

Let us define precognition. "Pre" means "before," and "cognition" means "knowing." Therefore, precognition means to know something before it happens.

There are many reports of people who spontaneously made a decision that saved their life - for example, *not* boarding their flight, *not* pulling forward at an intersection when the light turned green, etc. In cases like those, people soon received confirmation that their instincts were spot on, even if they didn't understand them. The plane crashed, or a drunk driver ran the red light. If you had pulled forward...

In some circles, it's understood that precognition spontaneously occurs as a self-protective mechanism. Some part of our mind is deeply concerned with guarding against life-threatening situations. It seems it's willing to look into the future and scan for approaching danger.

In my personal experience, there's a part of the mind concerned with interpersonal relationships as well. In high school and later in college, I had dreams where both girlfriends were physically intimate with other guys.

In both cases, I confronted the girls as soon as I could. And, guiltily, each of them verified the accuracy of my dreams. I was even correct about the guys they had been with. My life hadn't been at risk, but I suffered heartbreak in each case.

I share these examples to indicate an essential principle about precognition and psychic phenomena in general. One's mind must be keenly invested in obtaining the information, either consciously or subconsciously. It has to *matter* to you. Adding the element of *fun* is a way to make things matter.[62]

Precognition can be done by yourself or with the assistance of a friend. It is assumed you'll choose a target you've already learned to perceive. Trying to accomplish precognition with numbers doesn't make sense if you haven't done Phase 8 yet.

Suppose you're just starting with this book and feel more excited about doing precognition with numbers than anything else. In that case, it's time to "go rogue." Go straight to Phase 8, and incorporate the

---

[62] You can apply this concept to other parts of your life. Is your relationship stale? Is your job tedious? Are you in a funk? Take your spouse or partner on a fun adventure. Turn an aspect of your job into a game or competition. Treat yourself to a class, a performance, or a hiking trail you've never experienced before. Many aspects of our lives suffer when we don't' experience variety.

precognition exercise below once you've developed some accuracy perceiving numbers.

**Extra material required**: a large envelope or folder to conceal a single card

<u>By Yourself</u>

Step 1. Whether using colors, shapes, letters or numbers, shuffle your cards while blindfolded. Then, randomly select one of them and place it inside the envelope or folder.

Step 2. You can remove your blindfold, and place the envelope in another room.

Step 3. Go about your day, and try not to think about what's in the envelope.

Step 4. Later on, sit down in your usual training area. Go through your relaxation process while wearing your blindfold. When you're ready, intend to perceive the card you'll see in the next few minutes. You can imagine it in the space in front of your face, or lying on the table in front of you. You might tell your mind, "Show me the card I will see in a few minutes."

Step 5. Record your impressions on paper.

Step 6. Remove your blindfold, and bring the envelope from the other room back to your training area, where you sat before.

Step 7. Open the envelope, mentally marking <u>now</u> as the specific *moment* you intended to perceive.

After you take the card out of the envelope, you might alternate holding it in front of your face with placing it on the table in front of you while you stare at it.

You might also incorporate a bit of "self-telepathy" by intending to mentally *send* the color to your past self, to the "you" who was sitting in that chair just a few minutes ago.

## With a Partner

The whole process remains the same as above, except that your partner will shuffle, select, and hide the card for you. To prevent you from reading your partner's mind, your partner should blindfold themselves as they shuffle and hide the card, so they are also unaware of what's inside the envelope. When it's time to reveal the card, you can do it by yourself, or your partner can bring the envelope to you.

Your partner can make this more interesting by using a three-dimensional object instead of a card. Have them select a random object and place it in the same room they would have kept the envelope in until the time comes to reveal it to you.

## Adding "Temporal Stability" to Your Experiment

What I am about to share is a *belief* I have based on my experience. I cannot prove it; it's only a hypothesis. I believe small and quick events in the future are more difficult to perceive than large and long-lasting ones.

For example, suppose the probability of one football team winning over the other tomorrow is overwhelming. In that case, predicting who the winner will be is relatively easy. But let's say you're trying to predict (without influencing) the next flip of a coin, or whether a roulette number will be red or black, or which Bingo ball will be pulled from the basket. These are small, very quick occurrences in space-time. They're highly unstable. While certain future events may be stable, small events like these are highly random and insignificant. And, they don't do much to affect their surrounding reality.

Keeping the randomly selected card or object in a separate room for several hours or days adds the element of "*experimental* temporal stability." It takes the randomness out of the experiment.

As you send your mind into the future, there's no risk of the future shifting enough to change which target you'll be shown. If today's target inside the envelope is a blue triangle, then tomorrow, it will still be a blue triangle. This is *experimental* temporal stability.

On the other hand, if you attempt to perceive five targets in the same sitting, only a couple of minutes in between them, confusion arises. How will you respond if you think the first card will be yellow but turns out to be red? And what if the *second* card you attempt to predict a couple of minutes later turns out to be yellow? Were you just wrong the first time? Or did your mind skip several minutes further into the future and perceive the right card but the wrong *time*?

Therefore, injecting significant time between each precognition experiment is valuable for evaluating your experience and improving your accuracy. It removes the excuse of "Oh, I accidentally perceived the next card instead of *this* card." Doing one experiment per day is your best bet.

# PRECOGNITION AND THE LOTTERY[63]

Once you've developed yourself with single number targets (in combination with Phase 8), you may want to challenge yourself with complex targets involving more than one number at a time. Three-number lotteries are a great tool to use. Many regions offer a "Pick 3" lottery or something similar. Three numbers are drawn, between 0 and 9. It's possible for the same number to be drawn twice.

There's no need to purchase a lottery ticket to do this training, although doing so can add excitement.

Required materials

A. The large number printouts for numbers 0 through 9 from the Phase 8 download page on **www.learnmindsight.com/phase8.html.**

B. Three blank sheets of paper and tape to stick them on a wall.

C. A pen or pencil and a single piece of paper.

Steps

Step 1. Determine what day and time the next Pick-3 (or similar) lottery will be drawn. If your local lottery uses five or six numbers, focus on the first three numbers and ignore the rest. If you become adept at this exercise, then you can adapt it to perceive four, five, or six numbers over time.

---

[63] If you're particularly interested in lottery prediction, I recommend the book *Associative Remote Viewing: The Art & Science of Predicting Outcomes for Sports, Politics, Finances and the Lottery* by Debra Lynn Katz and Jon Knowles.

Step 2. Determine three rooms in your home where you can sit down and comfortably gaze at a blank spot on the wall. For example, a bedroom, a living room, and a dining room.

Step 3. Hang, place, or tape a piece of blank paper on the wall of each room, at a height even with your gaze.

Step 4. In room #1, put on your blindfold and go through your preparation. Then, direct your mind to perceive which number you will see on that wall tomorrow evening. Write down what number you think it is.

**Important:** Your intention should NOT be to "perceive tonight's winning lottery numbers." Instead, you should be focusing on seeing the numbers which will be placed on the wall and remain there all of the following day. Of course, these are **the same** as the winning numbers, but this is about the *process* of perceiving them and how to structure one's intention.

Step 5. Repeat the process inside room #2 and #3. If you can safely move from room to room with your blindfold on, then that will reduce your preparation time in the other rooms. A partner can guide you to each room. If you're by yourself, then remove your blindfold so you can walk safely. Repeat your preparation in each new room.

Step 6. When you are done, you will have written down three numbers. If you feel like it, go buy a ticket for tonight's drawing.

Step 7. After the winning numbers are posted on the lottery's website, hang the printout of the *first* winning number, replacing the blank paper in room #1. For the *second* winning number, repeat the process in room #2, and the same for the *third* winning number in room #3.

For this example, let's assume you'll do your precognition this afternoon. The lottery drawing will be this evening. Then, you'll hang up the actual winning numbers either tonight or first thing in the morning, *leaving them up all day* tomorrow. This creates a second type of temporal stability, "*experiential* temporal stability."[64]

Leaving the numbers on the walls for an entire day (the day after the lottery is drawn) gives your mind options for time travel. Let's say the winning number you placed on the wall in your dining room is 9.

---

[64] The first type of temporal stability (experimental) is discussed in the section above, Practicing Precognition.

When you do your precognition session in the dining room and send your mind into the future to see which number is posted on the wall the next day, your mind can travel to 9:00 a.m., noon, 3:00 p.m., etc.

No matter what time of day your mind visits the dining room tomorrow, the number 9 will always be there. This adds stability to your mind's experience, which is why I call this "*experiential* temporal stability." Again, this is only a hypothesis. Even though it might be faulty, it acts as a model to work with.

# PRACTICING RETROCOGNITION

Retrocognition is perceiving events which occurred in the past. The training process is similar to precognition, except for the order of some of the steps. In this exercise, we'll include a partner from the start.

Step 1. Your partner will randomly select a color while blindfolded, then, without looking at it, place it in an envelope.

Step 2. Your partner will place it on the table in your training area, or some place you are familiar with. No other training materials should be inside that room, especially on the table.

Step 3. For that whole day, you should avoid the same room the envelope is being kept in.

Step 4. That evening or early the next morning, your partner will move the envelope to another room. Ideally, you won't know where they put it.

Step 5. The following day, you'll sit in your training area and do your preparation, including wearing your blindfold.

Step 6. Set your intention, directing your mind to show you which card rested on that table **the previous day**.

Step 7. Record your impressions, then ask your partner to take you to where the card is currently being kept. Then, open the envelope and see how you did.

# LONG-DISTANCE PERCEPTION & TELEPATHY

Long-distance perception is a direct way to differentiate between dermo-optical perception and clairvoyance. Since the target will be in another room or in a box, your skin sensors won't be able to perceive light from it. Therefore, your consistent ability to identify the target from another room will be evidence for clairvoyance.

## PRACTICING LONG-DISTANCE PERCEPTION

Step 1. You or your partner will randomly select a card the way you did in the precognition and retrocognition exercises above.

Step 2: If you're by yourself - Place the card inside a box, and close the lid. Then place the box on the table in front of you.

If you have a partner - They will take the card to another room, place it on a table, and close the door. If they can do this without seeing what color (or shape, etc.) the card it, that will eliminate the possibility of telepathy being used.

Step 3: After you spend time preparing yourself, direct your attention toward the target with the intention of perceiving it.

Step 4: Record your impressions, then look inside the box, or walk to the other room and look at the card.

NOTE: If you plan on doing several long-distance experiments in one day, you can help yourself by keeping your blindfold on the whole time. Instead of seeing the target with your eyes, you can feel the glued letters in the center of the card to know what color it is[65]. Or, if you have a partner, they can look at the card themselves and *tell* you what it is.

---

[65] Gluing a letter or letters into the center of each card allows you to know its color without removing your blindfold. This technique is discussed in Part 3.

# PRACTICING TELEPATHY

Telepathy is composed of two words. "pathy" is defined as "feeling or suffering," and "tele" means "distant" or "over a distance."[66] For us, we can define it as perceiving another person's *experience*. While training, that person can be in front of you, across town, or in another city. Many parapsychologists and psychics will agree that physical distance poses no obstacle to the transmission of information.

Obviously, you'll need a partner for this exercise. Your partner should be familiar with the same types of targets that you are using. For this example, we'll assume you're both practicing Phase 6, shapes.

An important consideration is the need to separate telepathy from clairvoyance. Let's say you are preparing to read your friend's mind, and you're using a Zoom or Skype session since you live in different countries. Your friend has shuffled a set of papers with shapes on them and selected one to focus on while you read their mind.

They know you can't see the paper on their table since the camera is directed at their face. But what is there to prevent your consciousness from perceiving the paper shape on their table instead of perceiving your friend's *visualization* of that shape? Nothing! At least, there's currently no sure way to tell exactly how your mind gained the information.

To ensure that telepathy is being used instead of clairvoyance, your friend will need to decide which shape they want to hold in their mind ahead of time. Also, they should remove all targets from their room. The visualization of the target image inside their head will be your only source of information at that point.

As usual, put on your blindfold and go through your preparation. When you're ready to begin, ask your partner to start visualizing the shape. The word "visualization" implies a visual experience as if they were *seeing* the shape. However, we're interested in a variety of sensory experiences. Suppose their chosen shape is a black triangle. In that case, they can also mentally repeat "black triangle!" with their *inner voice* while imagining how it appears. You might *hear* the words "black" and "triangle" instead of seeing one.

Your partner could also keep the *feeling* of the shape in mind. While visualizing the shape, they might enhance the feeling of the "pointy-ness" of the triangle's three corners, the "roundness" of a circle, the "boxy-ness" of a square, etc. As the perceiver, you might have sessions where you *feel* the target instead of seeing it.

---

[66] Merriam-Webster's Dictionary

Of course, your mind can also translate their knowledge of the black triangle as just a "knowing." You'll have times when *you just know* what it is.

Suppose they've steadily trained from Phase 1 to Phase 6. In that case, they will have gradually developed the ability to keep their attention on their visualization for an extended period, which will help.

There are different ways to experiment with your telepathy. As with many of the other exercises, you could direct your mind with a basic intention. In this case, to "see what shape my partner is thinking about."

You could also add an element of neural targeting. A lot of visual processing occurs in the occipital lobe of the brain. This is located just inside the base of the skull, the large bump above the back of the neck. So, you might experiment with directing your intention toward that part of their brain as part of your process.

However, visualization occurs as a process involving multiple parts of the brain, such as the frontal, parietal, and temporal lobes.[67] Interestingly, some people experience visualization occurring in the space behind their forehead, which some refer to as their "third eye." This is in the region of the frontal lobe. Therefore, you could also experiment with pointing your intention toward the space just inside their forehead and see what kind of results you get.

The question arises, "How is focusing on a certain part of the brain, which is just a lump of wet flesh, supposed to reveal an image?" That's true. If we sliced open someone's frontal lobe, we wouldn't find a black triangle waiting there.

Focusing on a specific part of our partner's head can serve as a *focal point* for our attention. Sustaining attention to an experience for an extended period is helped by using a focal point.

And we can also be open to the possibility these portions of the brain are *physically* responding to an experience of *non-physical* consciousness. The electrical and chemical impulses are only half the story, the physical half. The other half involves the non-physical mind. Tuning into the physical brain might serve as an access point to their non-physical mind, like a special transducer making telepathy possible.[68]

---

[67] Neuroscience News. (August 27, 2015). *Have Trouble Visualizing Images? You May Have Aphantasia.* Retrieved from https://neurosciencenews.com/aphantasia-visualizing-images-2514/

[68] For more on telepathy, read "Mind to Mind" by René Warcollier (see Recommended Reading)

The most important thing to remember is as long as you keep experimenting in various ways, you'll find a way that works for you. And it might differ from anything you've read here. This is just a starting point.

# PART 3

# THE TRAINING

# REQUIRED MATERIALS

The materials listed below can be found at your local hobby, craft, or office supplies store:

## For All Phases

#1: A bottle of Elmer's glue with the nozzle on it. Actually, any glue that can be drawn onto paper and leave a thick line when dried is acceptable.

#2: Speakers or headphones, and a device for listening to the online meditations and timing tracks.

#3: A smart phone, laptop, or desktop for accessing the website and for using the Digital Color Wheel, discussed earlier in Preparatory Exercises.

## For Phases 1 Through 4

#1: 10 sheets of each color on full-size paper (or colored foam cards). I refer to colored paper, paper printouts, and foam cards alike as "cards" throughout the book. These are the following colors:

white
black
red
yellow
blue
green

As you get accustomed to the training, you can add other colors. It is important to get the **same type (texture) of paper** for all colors. If you can feel the difference, for example between the blue and red papers, with the skin of your fingers, this will render the exercise useless.

#2: A blindfold which completely blocks out light.[69]

---

[69] The "Mindfold" brand is a popular choice, but there are others such as "MZOO," "Manta," and "Bucky." They all generally allow you to open your eyes with the blindfold on, which you may prefer to do during your training.

## A Note About Blindfolds

In my experience, blindfolds **do not** always prevent light from entering them. I needed to apply some black electrician's tape onto my blindfold just over the bridge of my nose because it was an area that periodically allowed light inside.

Also, if the ambient light is bright enough, or if a card I'm holding is reflecting light from a bright nearby lamp, the light can penetrate the foam edges of the blindfold. For this reason, I prefer to train with my eyes closed beneath the blindfold and apply dark tape anywhere there may be leakages. I also enjoy practicing at night with the lights off.

As you'll find out, light leakage ruins the experience and can be frustrating. Nobody is here to fool themselves by peeking through their blindfold.

## Optional Materials for Phases 1 Through 4

From the earlier section, How to Use This Book, Cross Training and Boredom Busters: "balls, solid-colored paper (gift) bags, plastic cups, flowers, balloons, etc."

## For Phase 5

A printer (you'll print resources from the book's website) OR white paper and a black marker with a wide tip.

## For Phase 6

A printer OR white paper and a black marker with a broad tip. But in this phase, a printer will be much easier and time-conserving.

## For Phase 7

A **color printer**. Or, you can cut shapes from colored paper and glue them onto white paper. For this, you'll need a compass to draw circles, and a ruler or straight-edge for the other shapes.

## For Phases 8 Through 14

All the same supplies as before.

# THE GLUE TECHNIQUE

When I first began training myself, I struggled with a couple of different methods to check my accuracy. I needed a way to know if the card I was holding was the same color I thought it was or if the shape on it was actually a triangle when I perceived it to be.

The first method I used was simply checking by lifting my blindfold to peak at the card and see. The downside was that I'd spent significant time letting my eyes get used to the darkness before starting a session. Now I had to spoil it by exposing them to light every few minutes.

The next method I used was to download a smartphone app. It was designed to help visually impaired people identify colors and objects. After hovering my phone over a card for a few moments, a voice would begin to repeat the color, "Yellow... yellow... yellow." I continued until I pressed a small arrow on the screen to make it end. There were a couple of problems with this. Finding the arrow without using my eyes was often difficult and became a minor cause of stress. The other problem was sometimes the app was wrong. For example, it would call a yellow card "blue" or an orange card "red." The last thing I needed was to confuse my brain by labeling colors incorrectly.

I needed a simple and dependable way to identify a card's color. At one point, I had glued popsicle sticks onto some cards because I was worried about feeling the differences in the paper. I noticed the heavy texture of the dried glue and realized my solution. If I glued letters in the middle of each card to identify its color, I could run my fingers over it and know. Only later did I realize I was using a similar premise as Braille.

As long as your letters are similar in size and small enough, you won't accidentally touch them as long as you make a point to hold cards close to their edges.

You can choose any labeling system that you prefer. Here's how I labeled my cards, using a combination of upper and lower case letters. This works on paper and foam:

- black      Bk
- blue       bL
- Red        R
- Yellow     Y
- Green      g
- White      W

Instructions for using glue for working with contrast, shapes, numbers, and letters will be provided during those phases.

**BE SURE TO MAKE A **THICK** GLUE LINE BECAUSE IT SHRINKS WHILE DRYING. FOAM AND GLOSSY PAPER WORK BETTER THAN NORMAL PRINTING PAPER SINCE THEY'RE LESS ABSORBENT

Using glue to put textured letters on cards.
Allow the glue to dry overnight before using.

# WORKING WITH COLOR

Mind Sight is a process of self-discovery. Releasing one particular belief will especially help you embark on your journey. This is the belief that you'll perceive your card by holding it directly in front of your blindfolded eyes. Your eyes are no longer involved with perception, but out of habit, you might tend to hold your card there instead of trying other places.

Suppose the principle of dermo-optical perception is at work. In that case, we should remember that we are completely wrapped in skin. The skin on the back of our neck can perceive, as can the skin over our collar bones or our cheeks. This is a 360-degree opportunity.

If the principle of non-physical perception is at work instead, then we don't quite know where the source of perception is. It could be our entire nervous system which serves as a psychic antenna.

While working with the cards, you should experiment by holding them near different parts of your head and body. You can try:

- Holding the card still in one location for a period of time

- Tilting the angle of the card back and forth over one particular location

- Waving the card over the same location

- Slowly waving the card back and forth between two locations

Some people refer to "windows" of perceptions opening up in specific areas of their heads. Some areas are more sensitive than others.

Your tasks include:

- Becoming sensitized to how different parts of your body feel when exposed to each card

- Learning which of your "windows" are consistently open and reliable

- Becoming vigilant about visual, auditory, and other impressions arising in your awareness while intending to perceive the card you're holding.

Below are examples of how you can explore each card. Note that one of the cards is held in front of the lower part of the torso. In another image below, the subject is using the palm of his hand to sense the card.

# Windows of Perception

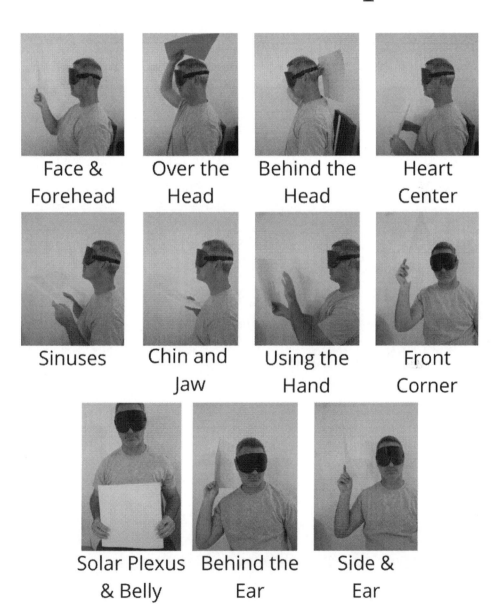

| Face & Forehead | Over the Head | Behind the Head | Heart Center |

| Sinuses | Chin and Jaw | Using the Hand | Front Corner |

| Solar Plexus & Belly | Behind the Ear | Side & Ear |

# USING THE TRAINING JOURNAL

Each phase is followed by a training journal. Each individual entry is intended for a single session. When you have completed each session for that phase's journal, you'll be ready to move on to the next phase.

If you decide to "go rogue," you might leave a phase early and start on another one. It will still be helpful for you to mark which sessions you've completed so you can return to unfinished ones if you decide you need to "go back to the basics," or if it adds more variety for you.

Each journal entry will:

- Tell you which specific cards or downloadable materials to use

- Have a space for you to record your experience during the session briefly. If you are prolific, you can use a blank notebook.

Recording your experiences, especially your state of mind, will enhance your personal growth process. Some days will be easier or more productive than others. By looking back over your journal, you'll learn what conditions are most helpful for you.

EXAMPLES OF WHAT YOU MIGHT RECORD

- What significant impressions did you receive?

- What was your state of mind or level of energy before you started?

- How did you feel throughout the session?

- How did you feel after the session?

- Is there anything you'd like to celebrate?

- What would you like to remember for next time?

- How could you improve your approach or attitude?

# PHASE 1 - COLOR FAMILIARIZATION

Phase 1 assumes you've spent several days or weeks using the materials from the chapter Preparatory Exercises.

This phase is entirely focused on familiarization. You will patiently be training your mind to relate a card's impressions with the name of a color. You'll know when you're holding a red card, for example. As you work with it, you'll automatically train your brain to relate those impressions to "red."

You'll also use differentiation to assist your learning process. Each session will use two colors. You'll learn about each color in part by discovering how they feel distinct from each other. Obviously, in time they'll differ by what color arises in your mental screen. But there are other ways you'll perceive them.

A color might provoke a certain mood in you. It could cause physical sensations on your skin, in your bones, or even in your teeth. When these sensations occur, you can be confident you're perceiving the card. By reminding your brain that this card is "red," it'll eventually respond by projecting the appropriate color into your mind.

SESSION LENGTH
Each Phase 1 session is around an hour long. The first 20 minutes will be spent either listening to one of the online meditations, doing your own relaxation exercise, or simply relaxing while acclimating to wearing the blindfold. **The blindfold should be worn for the entire session.**

THREE ROUNDS OF ALTERNATING COLORS AND RESTING BETWEEN THEM
Note: You can listen to a guided timer to use specifically for Phase 1. That way, you don't need to see a timer with your eyes to do this. Find the timer at **www.learnmindsight.com/phase1.html**

- Round 1: You'll work with the first color for 5 minutes, then rest for 5 minutes, then repeat with the second color. My midbrain video tutorial offers ideas for how to spend your rest periods.

- Round 2: You'll do the same, but instead of 5 minutes, each segment will last 4 minutes.

- Round 3: Same as above, but with segments lasting 3 minutes each.

Don't forget to include boredom busters[70] when necessary.

---

[70] From How to Use This Book

SESSION 1      Use 1 RED card and 1 BLUE card
DATE:          Personal Notes, Experiences, Reminders:




SESSION 2      Use 1 WHITE card and 1 BLUE card
DATE:          Personal Notes, Experiences, Reminders:




SESSION 3      Use 1 GREEN card and 1 BLUE card
DATE:          Personal Notes, Experiences, Reminders:

SESSION 4      Use 1 YELLOW card and 1 BLUE card
DATE:          Personal Notes, Experiences, Reminders:

SESSION 5      Use 1 BLACK card and 1 BLUE card
DATE:          Personal Notes, Experiences, Reminders:

SESSION 6      Use 1 RED card and 1 WHITE card
DATE:          Personal Notes, Experiences, Reminders:

SESSION 7      Use 1 BLUE card and 1 WHITE card
DATE:          Personal Notes, Experiences, Reminders:

SESSION 8      Use 1 GREEN card and 1 WHITE card
DATE:          Personal Notes, Experiences, Reminders:

SESSION 9      Use 1 YELLOW card and 1 WHITE card
DATE:          Personal Notes, Experiences, Reminders:

SESSION 10     Use 1 BLACK card and 1 WHITE card
DATE:          Personal Notes, Experiences, Reminders:

SESSION 11     Use 1 BLUE card and 1 RED card
DATE:          Personal Notes, Experiences, Reminders:

SESSION 12     Use 1 GREEN card and 1 RED card
DATE:          Personal Notes, Experiences, Reminders:

SESSION 13    Use 1 YELLOW card and 1 RED card
DATE:         Personal Notes, Experiences, Reminders:

SESSION 14    Use 1 WHITE card and 1 RED card
DATE:         Personal Notes, Experiences, Reminders:

SESSION 15    Use 1 BLACK card and 1 RED card
DATE:         Personal Notes, Experiences, Reminders:

SESSION 16     Use 1 YELLOW card and 1 BLACK card
DATE:             Personal Notes, Experiences, Reminders:

SESSION 17     Use 1 BLUE card and 1 BLACK card
DATE:             Personal Notes, Experiences, Reminders:

SESSION 18     Use 1 WHITE card and 1 BLACK card
DATE:             Personal Notes, Experiences, Reminders:

SESSION 19    Use 1 RED card and 1 BLACK card
DATE:           Personal Notes, Experiences, Reminders:

SESSION 20    Use 1 GREEN card and 1 BLACK card
DATE:           Personal Notes, Experiences, Reminders:

SESSION 21    Use 1 RED card and 1 GREEN card
DATE:           Personal Notes, Experiences, Reminders:

SESSION 22    Use 1 BLUE card and 1 GREEN card
DATE:          Personal Notes, Experiences, Reminders:

SESSION 23    Use 1 WHITE card and 1 GREEN card
DATE:          Personal Notes, Experiences, Reminders:

SESSION 24    Use 1 BLACK card and 1 GREEN
DATE:          Personal Notes, Experiences, Reminders:

SESSION 25    Use 1 YELLOW card and 1 GREEN card
DATE:         Personal Notes, Experiences, Reminders:

SESSION 26    Use 1 BLACK card and 1 YELLOW card
DATE:         Personal Notes, Experiences, Reminders:

SESSION 27    Use 1 WHITE card and 1 YELLOW card
DATE:         Personal Notes, Experiences, Reminders:

SESSION 28   Use 1 GREEN card and 1 YELLOW card
DATE:        Personal Notes, Experiences, Reminders:

SESSION 29   Use 1 BLACK card and 1 YELLOW card
DATE:        Personal Notes, Experiences, Reminders:

SESSION 30   Use 1 RED card and 1 YELLOW card
DATE:        Personal Notes, Experiences, Reminders:

# Congratulations on Completing Phase 1

If you would like to be an active participant in this pilot program, you can do so by completing a quick online survey about your experience. If enough people participate, I'll be able to produce a revised edition to better assist future seers.

The survey can be completed with your name and email address, or anonymously. If you choose to do it anonymously, please remember the false name you use, so that you can use the same name in surveys for Phase 2, Phase 3, etc.. You'll leave the email address portion of the survey blank.

The Phase 1 survey will ask the following questions:

How many days passed from your first session to your last? This will indicate how many days you rested or took off in between sessions.

Which colors were easiest for you to perceive?

Which colors were most difficult for you to perceive?

Did you experience visual, auditory, tactile, or other impressions? If yes, please specify which types.

You can access the Phase 1 survey at
**www.learnmindsight.com/surveyphase1.html**

# PHASE 2 - TWO COLOR PERCEPTION

In Phase 2, you will combine perceiving a color <u>without</u> first knowing what it is with perceiving it <u>after learning</u> its identity by touching the glue letters. **You will need 20 cards** (papers or foam) total for each session. 10 will be of one color, 10 of the other.

<u>Step 1</u>

Shuffle the two colors of cards. You don't need to be blindfolded yet. The Phase 2 journal will tell you which colors to use in each session.

You can spread them out on a table and move them around, or use a large bag, "stirring," lifting and dropping the cards to mix them. Then place the pile of shuffled cards beneath your seat or to your side, but within easy reach. If you noticed what color the top card is, begin Step 2 by moving it to the middle of the pile while blindfolded.

<u>Step 2</u>
Relax with the blindfold on for 20 minutes. You can use the guided timer for Phase 2 at this point.
Find the timer at **www.learnmindsight.com/phase2.html**

<u>Step 3</u>
Work with the first card for **the first minute** without feeling the glue letters. Notice what arises in your perceptual field. Do not be concerned with figuring out what color it is.

<u>Step 4</u>
Start the **second minute** by feeling the glue letters to learn the card's color. Then continue working with that card. Now you know the perceptions you receive are related to "the color x." **You are training your brain** to associate your perceptions with specific colors.

<u>Step 5</u>
Set the card aside onto a "discard" pile, and **rest for 2 minutes** before picking up the next card and repeating these steps.

You will repeat this process for 40 minutes. Including the 20 minutes of relaxation, the whole session will last nearly an hour. The point is **not** to go through all 20 cards. We used that many for the purpose of randomization.

SESSION 1     Shuffle 10 RED cards and 10 BLUE cards
DATE:             Personal Notes, Experiences, Reminders:

SESSION 2     Shuffle 10 WHITE cards and 10 BLUE cards
DATE:             Personal Notes, Experiences, Reminders:

SESSION 3     Shuffle 10 GREEN cards and 10 BLUE cards
DATE:             Personal Notes, Experiences, Reminders:

SESSION 7     Shuffle 10 BLUE cards and 10 WHITE cards
DATE:        Personal Notes, Experiences, Reminders:

SESSION 8     Shuffle 10 GREEN cards and 10 WHITE cards
DATE:        Personal Notes, Experiences, Reminders:

SESSION 9     Shuffle 10 YELLOW cards and 10 WHITE cards
DATE:        Personal Notes, Experiences, Reminders:

SESSION 10       Shuffle 10 BLACK cards and 10 WHITE cards
DATE:            Personal Notes, Experiences, Reminders:

SESSION 11       Shuffle 10 BLUE cards and 10 RED cards
DATE:            Personal Notes, Experiences, Reminders:

SESSION 12       Shuffle 10 GREEN cards and 10 RED cards
DATE:            Personal Notes, Experiences, Reminders:

SESSION 13    Shuffle 10 YELLOW cards and 10 RED cards
DATE:        Personal Notes, Experiences, Reminders:

SESSION 14    Shuffle 10 WHITE cards and 10 RED cards
DATE:        Personal Notes, Experiences, Reminders:

SESSION 15    Shuffle 10 BLACK cards and 10 RED cards
DATE:        Personal Notes, Experiences, Reminders:

SESSION 16    Shuffle 10 YELLOW cards and 10 BLACK cards
DATE:         Personal Notes, Experiences, Reminders:

SESSION 17    Shuffle 10 BLUE cards and 10 BLACK cards
DATE:         Personal Notes, Experiences, Reminders:

SESSION 18    Shuffle 10 WHITE cards and 10 BLACK cards
DATE:         Personal Notes, Experiences, Reminders:

SESSION 19    Shuffle 10 RED cards and 10 BLACK cards
DATE:         Personal Notes, Experiences, Reminders:




SESSION 20    Shuffle 10 GREEN cards and 10 BLACK cards
DATE:         Personal Notes, Experiences, Reminders:




SESSION 21    Shuffle 10 RED cards and 10 GREEN cards
DATE:         Personal Notes, Experiences, Reminders:

SESSION 22     Shuffle 10 BLUE cards and 10 GREEN cards
DATE:          Personal Notes, Experiences, Reminders:

SESSION 23     Shuffle 10 WHITE cards and 10 GREEN cards
DATE:          Personal Notes, Experiences, Reminders:

SESSION 24     Shuffle 10 BLACK cards and 10 GREEN cards
DATE:          Personal Notes, Experiences, Reminders:

SESSION 25    Shuffle 10 YELLOW cards and 10 GREEN cards
DATE:         Personal Notes, Experiences, Reminders:

SESSION 26    Shuffle 10 BLACK cards and 10 YELLOW cards
DATE:         Personal Notes, Experiences, Reminders:

SESSION 27    Shuffle 10 WHITE cards and 10 YELLOW cards
DATE:         Personal Notes, Experiences, Reminders:

SESSION 28     Shuffle 10 GREEN cards and 10 YELLOW cards
DATE:          Personal Notes, Experiences, Reminders:

SESSION 29     Shuffle 10 BLACK cards and 10 YELLOW cards
DATE:          Personal Notes, Experiences, Reminders:

SESSION 30     Shuffle 10 RED cards and 10 YELLOW cards
DATE:          Personal Notes, Experiences, Reminders:

# Congratulations on Completing Phase 2

Thank you for continuing to be an active participant in this pilot program! Your input will greatly assist future seers.

The Phase 2 survey will ask the following questions:

Did your ability to perceive the card improve in general?

Was the timing of working with the cards and resting in between them just right? Or too long? Too short?

How many days passed from your first Phase 2 session to your last? This will indicate how many days you rested or took off in between sessions.

Which colors were easiest for you to perceive?

Which colors were most difficult for you to perceive?

Did you experience visual, auditory, tactile, or other impressions? If yes, please specify which types.

Did you discover a way to improve Phase 1 or Phase 2 to make it work better for you? And if so, what adjustments did you make?

You can access the Phase 2 survey at
**www.learnmindsight.com/surveyphase2.html**

# PHASE 3 - THREE COLOR PERCEPTION

Phase 3 is similar to Phase 2, except each session will use three different colors instead of two. You will **only need one card for each color**.

## Step 1
Have one card of each of the three colors you'll use for that session.

## Step 2
Relax with the blindfold on for 20 minutes. You can use the guided timer for Phase 3 at this point. Find the timer at **www.learnmindsight.com/phase3.html**

## Step 3
Shuffle the three cards. You might realize the color of the third card by simple elimination. However, this can serve as an "assist." While logically deducing its color, can you perceive the subtle impressions which accompany it?

## Step 4
Work with the first card for **the first minute** without feeling the glue letters. Notice what arises in your perceptual field. Do not be concerned with figuring out what color it is.

## Step 5
Start the **second minute** by feeling the glue letters to learn the card's color. Then continue working with that card. Now you know the perceptions you receive are related to "the color x." You are training your brain to associate your perceptions with specific colors.

## Step 6
Set the card aside onto a "discard" pile, and **rest for 2 minutes** before picking up the next card and repeating these steps for the second and third cards.

## Step 7
After working with the three cards, shuffle them again and repeat the cycle twice more.

You will repeat this process for approximately 40 minutes. Including the 20 minutes of relaxation, the whole session will last just over an hour.

SESSION 1     Shuffle RED, WHITE, BLUE cards (one of each)
DATE:          Personal Notes, Experiences, Reminders:

SESSION 2     Shuffle YELLOW, WHITE, BLUE cards (one of each)
DATE:          Personal Notes, Experiences, Reminders:

SESSION 3     Shuffle BLACK, WHITE, BLUE cards (one of each)
DATE:          Personal Notes, Experiences, Reminders:

SESSION 4      Shuffle GREEN, WHITE, BLUE cards (one of each)
DATE:          Personal Notes, Experiences, Reminders:

SESSION 5      Shuffle GREEN, WHITE, RED cards (one of each)
DATE:          Personal Notes, Experiences, Reminders:

SESSION 6      Shuffle YELLOW, WHITE, RED cards (one of each)
DATE:          Personal Notes, Experiences, Reminders:

SESSION 7      Shuffle BLACK, WHITE, RED cards (one of each)
DATE:           Personal Notes, Experiences, Reminders:

SESSION 8      Shuffle BLUE, WHITE, RED cards (one of each)
DATE:           Personal Notes, Experiences, Reminders:

SESSION 9      Shuffle BLUE, WHITE, BLACK cards (one of each)
DATE:           Personal Notes, Experiences, Reminders:

SESSION 10    Shuffle GREEN, WHITE, BLACK cards (one of each)
DATE:         Personal Notes, Experiences, Reminders:

SESSION 11    Shuffle RED, WHITE, BLACK cards (one of each)
DATE:         Personal Notes, Experiences, Reminders:

SESSION 12    Shuffle YELLOW, WHITE, BLACK cards (one of each)
DATE:         Personal Notes, Experiences, Reminders:

SESSION 13    Shuffle YELLOW, WHITE, GREEN cards (one of each)
DATE:             Personal Notes, Experiences, Reminders:

SESSION 14    Shuffle RED, WHITE, GREEN cards (one of each)
DATE:             Personal Notes, Experiences, Reminders:

SESSION 15    Shuffle BLACK, WHITE, GREEN cards (one of each)
DATE:             Personal Notes, Experiences, Reminders:

SESSION 16     Shuffle BLUE, WHITE, GREEN cards (one of each)
DATE:          Personal Notes, Experiences, Reminders:

SESSION 17     Shuffle BLUE, WHITE, YELLOW cards (one of each)
DATE:          Personal Notes, Experiences, Reminders:

SESSION 18     Shuffle BLACK, WHITE, YELLOW cards (one of each)
DATE:          Personal Notes, Experiences, Reminders:

SESSION 19    Shuffle GREEN, WHITE, YELLOW cards (one of each)
DATE:          Personal Notes, Experiences, Reminders:

SESSION 20    Shuffle RED, WHITE, YELLOW cards (one of each)
DATE:          Personal Notes, Experiences, Reminders:

SESSION 21    Shuffle RED, BLUE, WHITE cards (one of each)
DATE:          Personal Notes, Experiences, Reminders:

126

SESSION 22    Shuffle YELLOW, BLUE, WHITE cards (one of each)
DATE:           Personal Notes, Experiences, Reminders:

SESSION 23    Shuffle BLACK, BLUE, WHITE cards (one of each)
DATE:           Personal Notes, Experiences, Reminders:

SESSION 24    Shuffle GREEN, BLUE, WHITE cards (one of each)
DATE:           Personal Notes, Experiences, Reminders:

SESSION 25    Shuffle GREEN, BLUE, RED cards (one of each)
DATE:         Personal Notes, Experiences, Reminders:

SESSION 26    Shuffle YELLOW, BLUE, RED cards (one of each)
DATE:         Personal Notes, Experiences, Reminders:

SESSION 27    Shuffle BLACK, BLUE, RED cards (one of each)
DATE:         Personal Notes, Experiences, Reminders:

SESSION 28    Shuffle WHITE, BLUE, RED cards (one of each)
DATE:              Personal Notes, Experiences, Reminders:

SESSION 29    Shuffle WHITE, BLUE, BLACK cards (one of each)
DATE:              Personal Notes, Experiences, Reminders:

SESSION 30    Shuffle GREEN, BLUE, BLACK cards (one of each)
DATE:              Personal Notes, Experiences, Reminders:

SESSION 31     Shuffle RED, BLUE, BLACK cards (one of each)
DATE:          Personal Notes, Experiences, Reminders:


SESSION 32     Shuffle YELLOW, BLUE, BLACK cards (one of each)
DATE:          Personal Notes, Experiences, Reminders:


SESSION 33     Shuffle YELLOW, BLUE, GREEN cards (one of each)
DATE:          Personal Notes, Experiences, Reminders:

SESSION 34   Shuffle RED, BLUE, GREEN cards (one of each)
DATE:        Personal Notes, Experiences, Reminders:

SESSION 35   Shuffle BLACK, BLUE, GREEN cards (one of each)
DATE:        Personal Notes, Experiences, Reminders:

SESSION 36   Shuffle WHITE, BLUE, GREEN cards (one of each)
DATE:        Personal Notes, Experiences, Reminders:

SESSION 37    Shuffle WHITE, BLUE, YELLOW cards (one of each)
DATE:         Personal Notes, Experiences, Reminders:

SESSION 38    Shuffle BLACK, BLUE, YELLOW cards (one of each)
DATE:         Personal Notes, Experiences, Reminders:

SESSION 39    Shuffle RED, BLUE, YELLOW cards (one of each)
DATE:         Personal Notes, Experiences, Reminders:

SESSION 40    Shuffle GREEN, BLUE, YELLOW cards (one of each)
DATE:         Personal Notes, Experiences, Reminders:

SESSION 41    Shuffle RED, YELLOW, BLUE cards (one of each)
DATE:         Personal Notes, Experiences, Reminders:

SESSION 42    Shuffle WHITE, YELLOW, BLUE cards (one of each)
DATE:         Personal Notes, Experiences, Reminders:

SESSION 43     Shuffle BLACK, YELLOW, BLUE cards (one of each)
DATE:              Personal Notes, Experiences, Reminders:

SESSION 44     Shuffle GREEN, YELLOW, BLUE cards (one of each)
DATE:              Personal Notes, Experiences, Reminders:

SESSION 45     Shuffle GREEN, YELLOW, RED cards (one of each)
DATE:              Personal Notes, Experiences, Reminders:

SESSION 46    Shuffle WHITE, YELLOW, RED cards (one of each)
DATE:         Personal Notes, Experiences, Reminders:

SESSION 47    Shuffle BLACK, YELLOW, RED cards (one of each)
DATE:         Personal Notes, Experiences, Reminders:

SESSION 48    Shuffle BLUE, YELLOW, RED cards (one of each)
DATE:         Personal Notes, Experiences, Reminders:

SESSION 49    Shuffle BLUE, YELLOW, BLACK cards (one of each)
DATE:         Personal Notes, Experiences, Reminders:

SESSION 50    Shuffle GREEN, YELLOW, BLACK cards (one of each)
DATE:         Personal Notes, Experiences, Reminders:

SESSION 51    Shuffle RED, YELLOW, BLACK cards (one of each)
DATE:         Personal Notes, Experiences, Reminders:

SESSION 52    Shuffle WHITE, YELLOW, BLACK cards (one of each)
DATE:          Personal Notes, Experiences, Reminders:

SESSION 53    Shuffle WHITE, YELLOW, GREEN cards (one of each)
DATE:          Personal Notes, Experiences, Reminders:

SESSION 54    Shuffle RED, YELLOW, GREEN cards (one of each)
DATE:          Personal Notes, Experiences, Reminders:

SESSION 55    Shuffle BLACK, YELLOW, GREEN cards (one of each)
DATE:         Personal Notes, Experiences, Reminders:

SESSION 56    Shuffle BLUE, YELLOW, GREEN cards (one of each)
DATE:         Personal Notes, Experiences, Reminders:

SESSION 57    Shuffle BLUE, YELLOW, WHITE cards (one of each)
DATE:         Personal Notes, Experiences, Reminders:

SESSION 58    Shuffle BLACK, YELLOW, WHITE cards (one of each)
DATE:          Personal Notes, Experiences, Reminders:

SESSION 59    Shuffle GREEN, YELLOW, WHITE cards (one of each)
DATE:          Personal Notes, Experiences, Reminders:

SESSION 60    Shuffle RED, YELLOW, WHITE cards (one of each)
DATE:          Personal Notes, Experiences, Reminders:

SESSION 61    Shuffle YELLOW, RED, BLUE cards (one of each)
DATE:          Personal Notes, Experiences, Reminders:

SESSION 62    Shuffle WHITE, RED, BLUE cards (one of each)
DATE:          Personal Notes, Experiences, Reminders:

SESSION 63    Shuffle BLACK, RED, BLUE cards (one of each)
DATE:          Personal Notes, Experiences, Reminders:

SESSION 64   Shuffle GREEN, RED, BLUE cards (one of each)
DATE:        Personal Notes, Experiences, Reminders:

SESSION 65   Shuffle GREEN, RED, YELLOW cards (one of each)
DATE:        Personal Notes, Experiences, Reminders:

SESSION 66   Shuffle WHITE, RED, YELLOW cards (one of each)
DATE:        Personal Notes, Experiences, Reminders:

SESSION 67    Shuffle BLACK, RED, YELLOW cards (one of each)
DATE:            Personal Notes, Experiences, Reminders:

SESSION 68    Shuffle BLUE, RED, YELLOW cards (one of each)
DATE:            Personal Notes, Experiences, Reminders:

SESSION 69    Shuffle BLUE, RED, BLACK cards (one of each)
DATE:            Personal Notes, Experiences, Reminders:

SESSION 70    Shuffle GREEN, RED, BLACK cards (one of each)
DATE:          Personal Notes, Experiences, Reminders:

SESSION 71    Shuffle WHITE, RED, BLACK cards (one of each)
DATE:          Personal Notes, Experiences, Reminders:

SESSION 72    Shuffle YELLOW, RED, BLACK cards (one of each)
DATE:          Personal Notes, Experiences, Reminders:

SESSION 73    Shuffle WHITE, RED, GREEN cards (one of each)
DATE:          Personal Notes, Experiences, Reminders:

SESSION 74    Shuffle YELLOW, RED, GREEN cards (one of each)
DATE:          Personal Notes, Experiences, Reminders:

SESSION 75    Shuffle BLACK, RED, GREEN cards (one of each)
DATE:          Personal Notes, Experiences, Reminders:

SESSION 76    Shuffle BLUE, RED, GREEN cards (one of each)
DATE:           Personal Notes, Experiences, Reminders:

SESSION 77    Shuffle BLUE, RED, WHITE cards (one of each)
DATE:           Personal Notes, Experiences, Reminders:

SESSION 78    Shuffle BLACK, RED, WHITE cards (one of each)
DATE:           Personal Notes, Experiences, Reminders:

SESSION 79    Shuffle GREEN, RED, WHITE cards (one of each)
DATE:         Personal Notes, Experiences, Reminders:

SESSION 80    Shuffle YELLOW, RED, WHITE cards (one of each)
DATE:         Personal Notes, Experiences, Reminders:

SESSION 81    Shuffle YELLOW, BLACK, BLUE cards (one of each)
DATE:         Personal Notes, Experiences, Reminders:

SESSION 82    Shuffle WHITE, BLACK, BLUE cards (one of each)
DATE:         Personal Notes, Experiences, Reminders:

SESSION 83    Shuffle RED, BLACK, BLUE cards (one of each)
DATE:         Personal Notes, Experiences, Reminders:

SESSION 84    Shuffle GREEN, BLACK, BLUE cards (one of each)
DATE:         Personal Notes, Experiences, Reminders:

SESSION 85    Shuffle GREEN, BLACK, YELLOW cards (one of each)
DATE:              Personal Notes, Experiences, Reminders:

SESSION 86    Shuffle WHITE, BLACK, YELLOW cards (one of each)
DATE:              Personal Notes, Experiences, Reminders:

SESSION 87    Shuffle RED, BLACK, YELLOW cards (one of each)
DATE:              Personal Notes, Experiences, Reminders:

SESSION 88    Shuffle BLUE, BLACK, YELLOW cards (one of each)
DATE:         Personal Notes, Experiences, Reminders:

SESSION 89    Shuffle BLUE, BLACK, RED cards (one of each)
DATE:         Personal Notes, Experiences, Reminders:

SESSION 90    Shuffle GREEN, BLACK, RED cards (one of each)
DATE:         Personal Notes, Experiences, Reminders:

SESSION 91    Shuffle WHITE, BLACK, RED cards (one of each)
DATE:       Personal Notes, Experiences, Reminders:

SESSION 92    Shuffle YELLOW, BLACK, RED cards (one of each)
DATE:       Personal Notes, Experiences, Reminders:

SESSION 93    Shuffle WHITE, BLACK, GREEN cards (one of each)
DATE:       Personal Notes, Experiences, Reminders:

SESSION 94    Shuffle YELLOW, BLACK, GREEN cards (one of each)
DATE:         Personal Notes, Experiences, Reminders:

SESSION 95    Shuffle RED, BLACK, GREEN cards (one of each)
DATE:         Personal Notes, Experiences, Reminders:

SESSION 96    Shuffle BLUE, BLACK, GREEN cards (one of each)
DATE:         Personal Notes, Experiences, Reminders:

SESSION 97    Shuffle BLUE, BLACK, WHITE cards (one of each)
DATE:         Personal Notes, Experiences, Reminders:

SESSION 98    Shuffle RED, BLACK, WHITE cards (one of each)
DATE:         Personal Notes, Experiences, Reminders:

SESSION 99    Shuffle GREEN, BLACK, WHITE cards (one of each)
DATE:         Personal Notes, Experiences, Reminders:

SESSION 100   Shuffle YELLOW, BLACK, WHITE cards (one of each)
DATE:          Personal Notes, Experiences, Reminders:

# Congratulations on Completing Phase 3

Thank you for continuing to be an active participant in this pilot program! Your input will greatly assist future seers.

The Phase 3 survey will ask the following questions:

Did your ability to perceive the card improve in general?

Did you have any instances of your vision opening up suddenly or significantly?

Did you include boredom busters in your schedule? If so, how often?

Was the timing of working with the cards and resting in between them just right? Or too long? Too short?

How many days passed from your first Phase 3 session to your last? This will indicate how many days you rested or took off in between sessions.

Did you discover a way to improve Phase 3 to make it work better for you? And if so, what adjustments did you make?


You can access the Phase 3 survey at
**www.learnmindsight.com/surveyphase3.html**

# PHASE 4 - FIVE COLOR PERCEPTION

Phase 4 increases your autonomy by letting you choose how long to spend on each card. It will also increase the challenge by working with all five colors in each session.

You will need <u>three</u> cards for <u>each</u> of the five colors, fifteen total.

## Step 1
Relax with the blindfold on for 20 minutes. The Phase 4 timer only marks the beginning, middle, and end of the session. How much time you spend on each card is up to you. Find the timer at
**www.learnmindsight.com/phase4.html**

## Step 2
Shuffle the fifteen cards.

## Step 3
Work with the first card for as long as you'd like. Once you're confident about what color it is, check by feeling the glue letters in the center of the card.

## Step 4
Set the card aside onto a "discard" pile. Rest and clear your mind for few moments or minutes before moving on to the next card.

## Step 5
Continue patiently working with each card until the hour is finished. If you finish the cards before then and want to continue, reshuffle the cards in the discard pile and keep going. **If you seem to be going through the cards quickly, but inaccurately, read my **warning against guessing** in the chapter "Learn from My Mistakes."

Phase 4 has thirty sessions. Each session will last one hour (including the 20-minute relaxation period).

SESSION 1     ALL 5 COLORS, 3 OF EACH, SHUFFLED
DATE:         Personal Notes, Experiences, Reminders:

SESSION 2     ALL 5 COLORS, 3 OF EACH, SHUFFLED
DATE:         Personal Notes, Experiences, Reminders:

SESSION 3     ALL 5 COLORS, 3 OF EACH, SHUFFLED
DATE:         Personal Notes, Experiences, Reminders:

SESSION 4     ALL 5 COLORS, 3 OF EACH, SHUFFLED
DATE:          Personal Notes, Experiences, Reminders:

SESSION 5     ALL 5 COLORS, 3 OF EACH, SHUFFLED
DATE:          Personal Notes, Experiences, Reminders:

SESSION 6     ALL 5 COLORS, 3 OF EACH, SHUFFLED
DATE:          Personal Notes, Experiences, Reminders:

SESSION 7    ALL 5 COLORS, 3 OF EACH, SHUFFLED
DATE:        Personal Notes, Experiences, Reminders:

SESSION 8    ALL 5 COLORS, 3 OF EACH, SHUFFLED
DATE:        Personal Notes, Experiences, Reminders:

SESSION 9    ALL 5 COLORS, 3 OF EACH, SHUFFLED
DATE:        Personal Notes, Experiences, Reminders:

SESSION 10    ALL 5 COLORS, 3 OF EACH, SHUFFLED
DATE:        Personal Notes, Experiences, Reminders:

SESSION 11    ALL 5 COLORS, 3 OF EACH, SHUFFLED
DATE:        Personal Notes, Experiences, Reminders:

SESSION 12    ALL 5 COLORS, 3 OF EACH, SHUFFLED
DATE:        Personal Notes, Experiences, Reminders:

SESSION 13    ALL 5 COLORS, 3 OF EACH, SHUFFLED
DATE:         Personal Notes, Experiences, Reminders:




SESSION 14    ALL 5 COLORS, 3 OF EACH, SHUFFLED
DATE:         Personal Notes, Experiences, Reminders:




SESSION 15    ALL 5 COLORS, 3 OF EACH, SHUFFLED
DATE:         Personal Notes, Experiences, Reminders:

SESSION 16   ALL 5 COLORS, 3 OF EACH, SHUFFLED
DATE:            Personal Notes, Experiences, Reminders:

SESSION 17   ALL 5 COLORS, 3 OF EACH, SHUFFLED
DATE:            Personal Notes, Experiences, Reminders:

SESSION 18   ALL 5 COLORS, 3 OF EACH, SHUFFLED
DATE:            Personal Notes, Experiences, Reminders:

SESSION 19     ALL 5 COLORS, 3 OF EACH, SHUFFLED
DATE:         Personal Notes, Experiences, Reminders:

SESSION 20     ALL 5 COLORS, 3 OF EACH, SHUFFLED
DATE:         Personal Notes, Experiences, Reminders:

SESSION 21     ALL 5 COLORS, 3 OF EACH, SHUFFLED
DATE:         Personal Notes, Experiences, Reminders:

SESSION 22    ALL 5 COLORS, 3 OF EACH, SHUFFLED
DATE:          Personal Notes, Experiences, Reminders:

SESSION 23    ALL 5 COLORS, 3 OF EACH, SHUFFLED
DATE:          Personal Notes, Experiences, Reminders:

SESSION 24    ALL 5 COLORS, 3 OF EACH, SHUFFLED
DATE:          Personal Notes, Experiences, Reminders:

SESSION 25  ALL 5 COLORS, 3 OF EACH, SHUFFLED
DATE:    Personal Notes, Experiences, Reminders:

SESSION 26  ALL 5 COLORS, 3 OF EACH, SHUFFLED
DATE:    Personal Notes, Experiences, Reminders:

SESSION 27  ALL 5 COLORS, 3 OF EACH, SHUFFLED
DATE:    Personal Notes, Experiences, Reminders:

SESSION 28    ALL 5 COLORS, 3 OF EACH, SHUFFLED
DATE:          Personal Notes, Experiences, Reminders:

SESSION 29    ALL 5 COLORS, 3 OF EACH, SHUFFLED
DATE:          Personal Notes, Experiences, Reminders:

SESSION 30    ALL 5 COLORS, 3 OF EACH, SHUFFLED
DATE:          Personal Notes, Experiences, Reminders:

# Congratulations on Completing Phase 4

You are a great example of someone with patience, follow-through, and grit! Thank you for continuing to be an active participant in this pilot program. Your input will greatly assist future seers.

The Phase 4 survey will ask the following questions:

Was Phase 4 easier or more difficult than Phase 3?

By the time you finished, did your accuracy increase?

Do you feel like repeating Phase 2 or 3 again to train your brain more before continuing?

Did you do better when you spent more, or less time perceiving each card? And how much time would you estimate that was?

Did you have any instances of your vision opening up suddenly or significantly?

Did you include boredom busters in your schedule? If so, how often?

How many days passed from your first Phase 4 session to your last? This will indicate how many days you rested or took off in between sessions.

Did you discover a way to improve Phase 4 to make it work better for you? And if so, what adjustments did you make?

You can access the Phase 4 survey at
**www.learnmindsight.com/surveyphase4.html**

# PHASE 5 - Contrasting Black and White

Phase 5 focuses on your ability to differentiate black and white. This skill is essential for working with shapes, numbers, and letters.

There are four exercises, each one lasting seven days.

## EXERCISE ONE: BLACK SIDE/WHITE SIDE

Step 1

You will download 10 copies of the image below from
**www.learnmindsight.com/phase5.html**
Using small glue letters near the center of all 10 copies, mark one side as "W" and the other as "B"

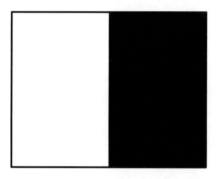

Step 2

Just like Phase 4, the Phase 5 timer will only mark the beginning, middle, and end of the session. Find the guided meditation and timer for the Phase 5 Exercises at **www.learnmindsight.com/phase5.html**

Step 3

During each session, you will shuffle the 10 copies on a table. Spin them around randomly so when you gather them into a pile, some will have the black side on the left, and others on the right. It doesn't have to be even.

Step 4

Leave one paper on the table, and set the rest on the floor or a side table.

Step 5

Wave your head or pass the palm of your hand over the paper. Try to determine which side is white, and which is black. Take as long as you need and then verify by feeling the glue letters near the center of the page. Then move on to the next one.

# EXERCISE TWO: BLACK DOT/WHITE DOT

Step 1
You will download 10 copies of the image below from
**www.learnmindsight.com/phase5.html**
Using small glue letters in the center of each circle, mark one as "W" and
the other as "B"

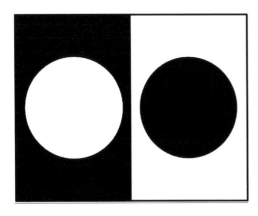

Step 2
Find the guided meditation and timer for Phase 5 Exercises at
**www.learnmindsight.com/phase5.html**

Step 3
During each session, you will shuffle the 10 copies on a table. Spin them
around randomly so when you gather them into a pile, some will have the
black circle on the left, and others on the right. It doesn't have to be even.

Step 4
Leave one paper on the table, and set the rest on the floor or a side table.

Step 5
Wave your head or pass the palm of your hand over the paper. Try to
determine which side has the white circle, and which has the black one. Take
as long as you need and then verify by feeling the glue letters inside the
circles. Then move on to the next one.

# EXERCISE THREE: HORIZONTAL LINE/VERTICAL LINE

Step 1
You will download 3 copies of <u>each</u> sheet pictured below from
**www.learnmindsight.com/phase5.html**

Place a small dot of glue on the ends of each line. Applying two layers of glue will ensure the dots are easy to feel while blindfolded.

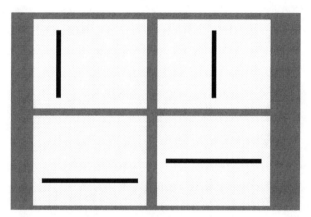

The four sheets for Exercise 3

Step 2
Find the guided meditation and timer for Phase 5 Exercises at
**www.learnmindsight.com/phase5.html**

Step 3
During each session, you will shuffle the twelve copies (three of each) together on a table. Spin them around randomly so when you gather them into a pile, you won't know which lines are centered on the page and which are offset.

Step 4
Leave one paper on the table, and set the rest on the floor or a side table.

Step 5
Wave your head or pass the palm of your hand over the paper. Try to determine where the line is on the paper. Take as long as you need and then verify by feeling the glue dots marking the ends of the line. Then move on to the next one.

# EXERCISE FOUR: STRAIGHT LINE/SQUIGGLY LINE

Step 1
You will download 5 copies <u>each</u> image below from
**www.learnmindsight.com/phase5.html**
- On the straight lines, you will place a small glue dot on each end (2 dots per line).
- On the squiggly line, you will do the same, and also place an additional dot near the center of the line (3 dots per line).

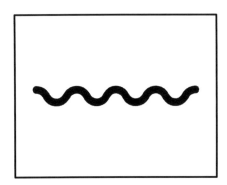 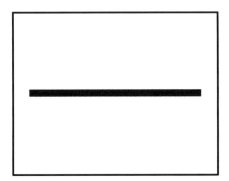

Step 2
Find the guided meditation and timer for Phase 5 Exercises at
**www.learnmindsight.com/phase5.html**

Step 3
During each session, you will shuffle the 10 copies on a table.

Step 4
Leave one paper on the table, and set the rest on the floor or a side table.

Step 5
Wave your head or pass your palm or fingers over the paper. Try to determine where the line is on the paper, and whether it is straight or squiggly. Take as long as you need and then verify by feeling the glue dots. You'll know it's squiggly if you feel the third dot near the center. Then move on to the next one.

SESSION 1 PHASE 5 - EXERCISE **ONE**
DATE: Personal Notes, Experiences, Reminders:

SESSION 2 PHASE 5 - EXERCISE ONE
DATE: Personal Notes, Experiences, Reminders:

SESSION 3 PHASE 5 - EXERCISE ONE
DATE: Personal Notes, Experiences, Reminders:

SESSION 4      PHASE 5 - EXERCISE ONE
DATE:          Personal Notes, Experiences, Reminders:

SESSION 5      PHASE 5 - EXERCISE ONE
DATE:          Personal Notes, Experiences, Reminders:

SESSION 6      PHASE 5 - EXERCISE ONE
DATE:          Personal Notes, Experiences, Reminders:

SESSION 7     PHASE 5 - EXERCISE ONE
DATE:         Personal Notes, Experiences, Reminders:

SESSION 8     PHASE 5 - EXERCISE **TWO**
DATE:         Personal Notes, Experiences, Reminders:

SESSION 9     PHASE 5 - EXERCISE TWO
DATE:         Personal Notes, Experiences, Reminders:

SESSION 10     PHASE 5 - EXERCISE TWO
DATE:         Personal Notes, Experiences, Reminders:

SESSION 11     PHASE 5 - EXERCISE TWO
DATE:         Personal Notes, Experiences, Reminders:

SESSION 12     PHASE 5 - EXERCISE TWO
DATE:         Personal Notes, Experiences, Reminders:

SESSION 13    PHASE 5 - EXERCISE TWO
DATE:         Personal Notes, Experiences, Reminders:




SESSION 14    PHASE 5 - EXERCISE TWO
DATE:         Personal Notes, Experiences, Reminders:




SESSION 15    PHASE 5 - EXERCISE **THREE**
DATE:         Personal Notes, Experiences, Reminders:

SESSION 16    PHASE 5 - EXERCISE THREE
DATE:          Personal Notes, Experiences, Reminders:

SESSION 17    PHASE 5 - EXERCISE THREE
DATE:          Personal Notes, Experiences, Reminders:

SESSION 18    PHASE 5 - EXERCISE THREE
DATE:          Personal Notes, Experiences, Reminders:

SESSION 19    PHASE 5 - EXERCISE THREE
DATE:         Personal Notes, Experiences, Reminders:


SESSION 20    PHASE 5 - EXERCISE THREE
DATE:         Personal Notes, Experiences, Reminders:


SESSION 21    PHASE 5 - EXERCISE THREE
DATE:         Personal Notes, Experiences, Reminders:

SESSION 22     PHASE 5 - EXERCISE **FOUR**
DATE:               Personal Notes, Experiences, Reminders:

SESSION 23     PHASE 5 - EXERCISE FOUR
DATE:               Personal Notes, Experiences, Reminders:

SESSION 24     PHASE 5 - EXERCISE FOUR
DATE:               Personal Notes, Experiences, Reminders:

SESSION 25     PHASE 5 - EXERCISE FOUR
DATE:          Personal Notes, Experiences, Reminders:

SESSION 26     PHASE 5 - EXERCISE FOUR
DATE:          Personal Notes, Experiences, Reminders:

SESSION 27     PHASE 5 - EXERCISE FOUR
DATE:          Personal Notes, Experiences, Reminders:

SESSION 28     PHASE 5 - EXERCISE FOUR
DATE:          Personal Notes, Experiences, Reminders:

# Congratulations on Completing Phase 5

You're doing great! Now things are going to get more interesting.

The Phase 5 survey will ask the following questions:

Was Phase 5 easier or more difficult than Phase 4?

Was the line easier for you to perceive, or the squiggle?

By the time you finished, did your accuracy increase?

Did you do better when you spent more, or less time perceiving each paper? And how much time would you estimate that was?

You can access the Phase 5 survey at
**www.learnmindsight.com/surveyphase5.html**

# PHASE 6 - SHAPES (Touching Paper)

Phase 6 focuses on your ability to differentiate between solid and hollow shapes. Also, it introduces a new aspect to Mind Sight training. Now, you can touch the paper and use your fingertips to help you perceive. You'll have a glue letter in the center of each image, so you'll need to be careful not to touch that part of the page. Since you'll be focusing on boundaries, you shouldn't need to move your fingers that far into the center.

There are 6 exercises, each one lasting 5 sessions.

Exercise One: Solid and hollow triangles

Exercise Two: Solid and hollow squares

Exercise Three: Solid and hollow circles

Exercise Four: Solid and hollow hearts

Exercise Five: Discerning all the solid shapes

Exercise Six: Discerning all the hollow shapes

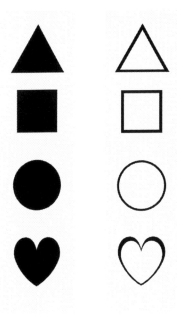

# INSTRUCTIONS FOR <u>ALL 6</u> EXERCISES

<u>Step 1</u>
Download 5 copies of all 6 images from
**www.learnmindsight.com/phase6.html**

In the center of each shape, you'll glue either the letter "H" for hollow, or "S" for solid. Make the letters small, but so that you are still able to read them with your fingertip.

<u>Step 2</u>
Find the guided meditation and timer for Phase 6 from
**www.learnmindsight.com/phase6.html**

<u>Step 3</u>
During each session, you will shuffle 10 copies for that session's shape (triangles one week, square next, etc.) on a table. Spin them around too.

<u>Step 4</u>
Leave one paper on the table, and set the rest on the floor or a side table.

<u>Step 5</u>
You can touch the paper with a fingertip. Working from the edge of the paper inward, perceive the edge of the shape. If the object is hollow, you may perceive a shift back to white after moving your finger in further. You can also lift it up and treat it like a color card. Be careful not to touch the small "H" or "S" in the center of the shape until you're ready to verify what it is. Take as long as you need. After having a brief rest, move on to the next one.

**\*\*NOTE: FOR EXERCISES 5 and 6 (starting with Session 21 in the journal)**

You will need to print new copies of the solid and hollow shapes to label them differently with glue. Instead of "S" and "H," you'll use "T" for triangle, "C" for circle, "S" for square, "H" for heart.

Since the <u>s</u>olid <u>s</u>quare already has an "S" in it and the <u>h</u>ollow <u>h</u>eart already has an "H" in it, you'll be able to reuse them instead of printing new ones.

SESSION 1　　PHASE 6 - **Exercise One** - Solid and hollow TRIANGLES
DATE:　　　　Personal Notes, Experiences, Reminders:

SESSION 2　　PHASE 6 - Exercise One - Solid and hollow TRIANGLES
DATE:　　　　Personal Notes, Experiences, Reminders:

SESSION 3　　PHASE 6 - Exercise One - Solid and hollow TRIANGLES
DATE:　　　　Personal Notes, Experiences, Reminders:

SESSION 4      PHASE 6 - Exercise One - Solid and hollow TRIANGLES
DATE:          Personal Notes, Experiences, Reminders:

SESSION 5      PHASE 6 - Exercise One - Solid and hollow TRIANGLES
DATE:          Personal Notes, Experiences, Reminders:

SESSION 6      PHASE 6 - **Exercise Two** - Solid and hollow SQUARES
DATE:          Personal Notes, Experiences, Reminders:

SESSION 7    PHASE 6 - Exercise Two - Solid and hollow SQUARES
DATE:        Personal Notes, Experiences, Reminders:

SESSION 8    PHASE 6 - Exercise Two - Solid and hollow SQUARES
DATE:        Personal Notes, Experiences, Reminders:

SESSION 9    PHASE 6 - Exercise Two - Solid and hollow SQUARES
DATE:        Personal Notes, Experiences, Reminders:

SESSION 10   PHASE 6 - Exercise Two - Solid and hollow SQUARES
DATE:        Personal Notes, Experiences, Reminders:




SESSION 11   PHASE 6 - **Exercise Three** - Solid and hollow CIRCLES
DATE:        Personal Notes, Experiences, Reminders:




SESSION 12   PHASE 6 - Exercise Three - Solid and hollow CIRCLES
DATE:        Personal Notes, Experiences, Reminders:

SESSION 13    PHASE 6 - Exercise Three - Solid and hollow CIRCLES
DATE:         Personal Notes, Experiences, Reminders:

SESSION 14    PHASE 6 - Exercise Three - Solid and hollow CIRCLES
DATE:         Personal Notes, Experiences, Reminders:

SESSION 15    PHASE 6 - Exercise Three - Solid and hollow CIRCLES
DATE:         Personal Notes, Experiences, Reminders:

SESSION 16     PHASE 6 - **Exercise Four** - Solid and hollow HEARTS
DATE:          Personal Notes, Experiences, Reminders:




SESSION 17     PHASE 6 - Exercise Four - Solid and hollow HEARTS
DATE:          Personal Notes, Experiences, Reminders:




SESSION 18     PHASE 6 - Exercise Four - Solid and hollow HEARTS
DATE:          Personal Notes, Experiences, Reminders:

SESSION 19    PHASE 6 - Exercise Four - Solid and hollow HEARTS
DATE:           Personal Notes, Experiences, Reminders:

SESSION 20    PHASE 6 - Exercise Four - Solid and hollow HEARTS
DATE:           Personal Notes, Experiences, Reminders:

SESSION 21    PHASE 6 - **Exercise Five** - Discerning between SOLID shapes
DATE:           Personal Notes, Experiences, Reminders:

SESSION 22     PHASE 6 - Exercise Five - Discerning between SOLID shapes
DATE:               Personal Notes, Experiences, Reminders:

SESSION 23     PHASE 6 - Exercise Five - Discerning between SOLID shapes
DATE:               Personal Notes, Experiences, Reminders:

SESSION 24     PHASE 6 - Exercise Five - Discerning between SOLID shapes
DATE:               Personal Notes, Experiences, Reminders:

SESSION 25    PHASE 6 - Exercise Five - Discerning between SOLID shapes
DATE:         Personal Notes, Experiences, Reminders:

SESSION 26    PHASE 6 - Exercise Five - Discerning between HOLLOW shapes
DATE:         Personal Notes, Experiences, Reminders:

SESSION 27    PHASE 6 - Exercise Five - Discerning between HOLLOW shapes
DATE:         Personal Notes, Experiences, Reminders:

SESSION 28    PHASE 6 - **Exercise Six** - Discerning between HOLLOW shapes
DATE:         Personal Notes, Experiences, Reminders:

SESSION 29    PHASE 6 - Exercise Six - Discerning between HOLLOW shapes
DATE:         Personal Notes, Experiences, Reminders:

SESSION 30    PHASE 6 - Exercise Six - Discerning between HOLLOW shapes
DATE:         Personal Notes, Experiences, Reminders:

# Congratulations on Completing Phase 6

Good job! You're getting even closer to reading without your eyes.

The Phase 6 survey will ask the following questions:

Were you able to perceive using your fingertip? Or did you rely on your head or hand? Or did you perceive some other way?

Was Phase 6 easier or more difficult than Phase 5?

By the time you finished, did your accuracy increase?

Do you have any suggestions for making Phase 6 better?

You can access the Phase 6 survey at
**www.learnmindsight.com/surveyphase6.html**

# PHASE 7 - COLORED SHAPES

Phase 7 combines shapes with colors. Like Phase 6, you can use your fingertips and touch the paper if you'd like. Just be careful not to touch the glue letters until you're ready to check.

Each session will use two shapes of different colors. You'll do two sessions with those particular shapes before working with a new set. You'll notice that only one of the shapes changes in order to use continuity to help you learn.

Overall, you'll spend 24 sessions in Phase 7.

These are the shapes you'll be working with:

- Black triangle
- Yellow square
- Blue circle
- Red heart

## INSTRUCTIONS

Step 1
You will need a color printer to download 5 copies of all 4 images from **www.learnmindsight.com/phase7.html**, otherwise you can use scissors to cut out shapes from colored paper and paste them onto white paper.

In the center of each shape, you'll glue either the letters "BT" for black triangle, "YS" for yellow square, "BC" for blue circle, and "Rh" for red heart. Make the letters small, but so that you are still able to read them with your fingertip.

Step 2
Find the guided meditation and timer for Phase 7 at **www.learnmindsight.com/phase7.html**

Step 3
During each session, you will shuffle 10 copies for that session's shapes (i.e. 5 black triangles and 5 yellow squares) on a table. Spin them around too.

Step 4
Leave one paper on the table, and set the rest on the floor or a side table.

Step 5
You can touch the paper with a fingertip as you did in Phase 6. You can also, pick it up and work with it the way you did in Phases 1, 2, 3, and 4.

Step 6
Take as long as you need, then feel the glue letters to verify. If you were incorrect, continue working with that shape for a few more minutes, so your brain will associate your impressions with it better.

Step 7
After having a brief rest, move on to the next one.

Note: Each exercise is repeated twice. For example, Session 1 and Session 2 are identical, as are Session 3 and 4, etc. If you perceive the cards clearly and see no benefit in repeating that specific session, feel free to move on to the next one.

SESSION 1     PHASE 7 - **Exercise One** - Yellow Square, Black Triangle
DATE:           Personal Notes, Experiences, Reminders:

SESSION 2     PHASE 7 - Exercise One - Yellow Square, Black Triangle
DATE:           Personal Notes, Experiences, Reminders:

SESSION 3     PHASE 7 - **Exercise Two** - Yellow Square, Blue Circle
DATE:           Personal Notes, Experiences, Reminders:

SESSION 4     PHASE 7 - Exercise Two - Yellow Square, Blue Circle
DATE:              Personal Notes, Experiences, Reminders:

SESSION 5     PHASE 7 - **Exercise Three** - Yellow Square, Red Heart
DATE:              Personal Notes, Experiences, Reminders:

SESSION 6     PHASE 7 - Exercise Three - Yellow Square, Red Heart
DATE:              Personal Notes, Experiences, Reminders:

SESSION 7    PHASE 7 - **Exercise Four** - Black Triangle, Yellow Square
DATE:         Personal Notes, Experiences, Reminders:

SESSION 8    PHASE 7 - Exercise Four - Black Triangle, Yellow Square
DATE:         Personal Notes, Experiences, Reminders:

SESSION 9    PHASE 7 - **Exercise Five** - Black Triangle, Blue Circle
DATE:         Personal Notes, Experiences, Reminders:

SESSION 10     PHASE 7 - Exercise Five - Black Triangle, Blue Circle
DATE:          Personal Notes, Experiences, Reminders:

SESSION 11     PHASE 7 - **Exercise Six** - Black Triangle, Red Heart
DATE:          Personal Notes, Experiences, Reminders:

SESSION 12     PHASE 7 - Exercise Six - Black Triangle, Red Heart
DATE:          Personal Notes, Experiences, Reminders:

SESSION 13    PHASE 7 - **Exercise Seven** - Red Heart, Blue Circle
DATE:         Personal Notes, Experiences, Reminders:

SESSION 14    PHASE 7 - Exercise Seven - Red Heart, Blue Circle
DATE:         Personal Notes, Experiences, Reminders:

SESSION 15    PHASE 7 - **Exercise Eight** - Red Heart, Yellow Square
DATE:         Personal Notes, Experiences, Reminders:

SESSION 16    PHASE 7 - Exercise Eight - Red Heart, Yellow Square
DATE:         Personal Notes, Experiences, Reminders:

SESSION 17    PHASE 7 - **Exercise Nine** - Red Heart, Black Triangle
DATE:         Personal Notes, Experiences, Reminders:

SESSION 18    PHASE 7 - Exercise Nine - Red Heart, Black Triangle
DATE:         Personal Notes, Experiences, Reminders:

SESSION 19    PHASE 7 - **Exercise Ten** - Blue Circle, Yellow Square
DATE:         Personal Notes, Experiences, Reminders:

SESSION 20    PHASE 7 - Exercise Ten - Blue Circle, Yellow Square
DATE:         Personal Notes, Experiences, Reminders:

SESSION 21    PHASE 7 - **Exercise Eleven** - Blue Circle, Black Triangle
DATE:         Personal Notes, Experiences, Reminders:

SESSION 22   PHASE 7 - Exercise Eleven - Blue Circle, Black Triangle
DATE:        Personal Notes, Experiences, Reminders:

SESSION 23   PHASE 7 - **Exercise Twelve** - Blue Circle, Red Heart
DATE:        Personal Notes, Experiences, Reminders:

SESSION 24   PHASE 7 - Exercise Twelve - Blue Circle, Red Heart
DATE:        Personal Notes, Experiences, Reminders:

# Congratulations on Completing Phase 7

Wonderful! Your persistence is paying off!

The Phase 7 survey will ask the following questions:

Was Phase 7 easier or more difficult than Phase 6?

Did you improve using your fingertip? Or did you improve any other way?

Do you have any suggestions for making Phase 7 better?

You can access the Phase 7 survey at
**www.learnmindsight.com/surveyphase7.html**

# PHASE 8 - NUMBERS

Now that you've spent several phases working on lines and curves, as well as using your fingertip, you're ready to begin working with numbers.

**PHASE 8 HAS THREE PARTS: A, B, C**

Part A: Familiarization Using Your Eyes

Step 1: Print out the large numbers from
**www.learnmindsight.com/phase8.html**

Step 2: At your own pace, for at least several days or weeks, work with one number at a time. Instead of using a blindfold, you'll look at the number with your eyes. Try to *feel* it as you look at it. Blink normally, of course. Then, close your eyes and see the number with your mind. Don't be concerned about whether or not you're actually perceiving it or using your memory.

Step 3: Also, work with using the palm of your hand, both touching the page and holding it just above the page. Feel the number both ways while your eyes are open and looking at it as well as while keeping your eyes closed for a few minutes.

Step 4: Experiment with exposing the paper to your "windows" around your head and body. Do so with your eyes open as well as closed. Whenever your eyes are open, direct your attention onto your inner mental perception. For example, if you're holding the card behind your head, your open eyes won't help in any way, forcing you to rely solely on your mental perception.

There are **no** journal entries for Part A since you'll decide how long to practice Part A on your own.

When you feel ready, continue to Part B.

Part B: Familiarization Similar to Phase 1

       Just like Phase 1, Phase 8 is entirely focused on familiarization. You will patiently train your mind to relate a card's impressions with a specific number. Each session assignment in the journal **will tell you** which two numbers to use. You'll know when you're holding the number 7, for example. As you work with it, you'll automatically train your brain to relate the impressions to "7."

       You'll also use differentiation to assist your learning process. Each session will use two numbers. You'll learn about each number partly by how distinct they feel from each other. Because of your previous work in Phases 5, 6, and 7, it's likely that you'll have strong visual impressions - that you'll _see_ the whole number, or _part_ of the number, directly.

       Each exercise is repeated twice. For example, Session 1 and Session 2 are identical, as are Session 3 and 4, etc. If you perceive the cards clearly and see no benefit in repeating that specific session, feel free to move on to the next one.

SESSION LENGTH

Each Part B session is around an hour long. The first 20 minutes will be spent either listening to one of the online meditations, doing your own preparatory exercise, or simply relaxing while adjusting to wearing the blindfold. **The blindfold should be worn for the entire session.**

THREE ROUNDS OF ALTERNATING NUMBERS AND RESTING BETWEEN THEM

Note: You can listen to a guided timer to use specifically for Part B. That way, you don't need to look at a timer to do this. Find the timer at **www.learnmindsight.com/phase8.html**

- Round 1: You'll work with the first number for 5 minutes, then rest for 5 minutes, then repeat with the second number.

- Round 2: You'll do the same, but instead of 5 minutes, each segment will last 4 minutes.

- Round 3: Same as above, but with segments lasting 3 minutes each.

As before, don't forget to include boredom busters when necessary.

## Part C: READING MEDIUM AND SMALL NUMBERS[71]

<u>Step 1</u>
Print out the medium and small number sheets from
**www.learnmindsight.com/phase8.html**

<u>Step 2</u>
Each print out has double-rows for each number. That is to say, beneath each number, you'll have space to draw the number above it with glue.

You'll also be able to draw over the gray boundary lines between the numbers with glue. The glue will need several hours to dry completely. If the paper absorbs the glue, **you may need to apply another layer to make it thick enough to feel.**

<u>Step 3</u>
You'll work on one sheet per session, starting with Sheet 1. Before working on a sheet, draw each number using glue in the empty cell beneath the number. This way, after working on a number for a while, you can verify your impressions by touching the glue.

In the beginning, the sheets will be so simple that you'll remember what numbers are on them, and this is good. You may even look at the sheet after it has dried, at the start of your session. This will help your brain relate to the impressions you'll receive after putting on your blindfold.

Work on each sheet for as long as it takes. Choose your preferred preparatory meditation or relaxation exercise to use before working on the sheet.

---

[71] I highly recommend you watch the month-long training videos on Wendy Gallant's YouTube channel in which Nikolay Denisov and Marina Kapirova trained her and Rob Freeman to read with fingers. Search YouTube using the term "Nikolay Denisov & Marina Teach Wendy Gallant, Rob Freeman"

Applying the glue numbers to Phase 8 Part C,
Sheet 1 for verifying while blindfolded

## USING YOUR FINGERTIP AS A GUIDE

You can also approach Step 3 differently. Instead of wearing your blindfold throughout the session, you can simply open and close your eyes as you work with each number. After you see the number with your open eyes, close them while keeping your finger tip next to the number or even on top of it. You'll need to experiment to see which way works best for you.

If you've been working your way through each Phase in sequence, you may have noticed yourself unexpectedly seeing the faint glow of your hands while holding up any of the cards. Or, you might have noticed the glow while using your hands and finger while working with the shape and line exercises of Phase 5 and Phase 6.

You can use your finger's glow to help you focus your preferred "window" onto the number you're working on. First, place your finger on the edge of the number. Then, become aware of your finger's glow. After you've established it, move your attention off of it and onto the paper to focus on the number. **You'll be able to apply this technique in all the remaining phases if you choose.**

SESSION 1      Part B: Use one "1" card and one "9" card
DATE:          Personal Notes, Experiences, Reminders:

SESSION 2      Part B: Use one "1" card and one "9" card
DATE:          Personal Notes, Experiences, Reminders:

SESSION 3      Part B: Use one "0" card and one "7" card
DATE:          Personal Notes, Experiences, Reminders:

SESSION 4    Part B: Use one "0" card and one "7" card
DATE:        Personal Notes, Experiences, Reminders:




SESSION 5    Part B: Use one "2" card and one "8" card
DATE:        Personal Notes, Experiences, Reminders:




SESSION 6    Part B: Use one "2" card and one "8" card
DATE:        Personal Notes, Experiences, Reminders:

SESSION 7          Part B: Use one "3" card and one "6" card
DATE:              Personal Notes, Experiences, Reminders:

SESSION 8          Part B: Use one "3" card and one "6" card
DATE:              Personal Notes, Experiences, Reminders:

SESSION 9          Part B: Use one "4" card and one "5" card
DATE:              Personal Notes, Experiences, Reminders:

SESSION 10   Part B: Use one "4" card and one "5" card
DATE:        Personal Notes, Experiences, Reminders:

SESSION 11   Part B: Use one "1" card and one "8" card
DATE:        Personal Notes, Experiences, Reminders:

SESSION 12   Part B: Use one "1" card and one "8" card
DATE:        Personal Notes, Experiences, Reminders:

SESSION 13      Part B: Use one "0" card and one "5" card
DATE:           Personal Notes, Experiences, Reminders:




SESSION 14      Part B: Use one "0" card and one "5" card
DATE:           Personal Notes, Experiences, Reminders:




SESSION 15      Part B: Use one "2" card and one "9" card
DATE:           Personal Notes, Experiences, Reminders:

SESSION 16     Part B: Use one "2" card and one "9" card
DATE:          Personal Notes, Experiences, Reminders:

SESSION 17     Part B: Use one "3" card and one "7" card
DATE:          Personal Notes, Experiences, Reminders:

SESSION 18     Part B: Use one "3" card and one "7" card
DATE:          Personal Notes, Experiences, Reminders:

SESSION 19    Part B: Use one "4" card and one "6" card
DATE:         Personal Notes, Experiences, Reminders:

SESSION 20    Part B: Use one "4" card and one "6" card
DATE:         Personal Notes, Experiences, Reminders:

SESSION 21    Part B: Use one "1" card and one "0" card
DATE:         Personal Notes, Experiences, Reminders:

SESSION 22     Part B: Use one "1" card and one "0" card
DATE:          Personal Notes, Experiences, Reminders:

SESSION 23     Part B: Use one "2" card and one "4" card
DATE:          Personal Notes, Experiences, Reminders:

SESSION 24     Part B: Use one "2" card and one "4" card
DATE:          Personal Notes, Experiences, Reminders:

SESSION 25    Part B: Use one "3" card and one "9" card
DATE:          Personal Notes, Experiences, Reminders:

SESSION 26    Part B: Use one "3" card and one "9" card
DATE:          Personal Notes, Experiences, Reminders:

SESSION 27    Part B: Use one "8" card and one "7" card
DATE:          Personal Notes, Experiences, Reminders:

SESSION 28    Part B: Use one "8" card and one "7" card
DATE:         Personal Notes, Experiences, Reminders:

SESSION 29    Part B: Use one "5" card and one "6" card
DATE:         Personal Notes, Experiences, Reminders:

SESSION 30    Part B: Use one "5" card and one "6" card
DATE:         Personal Notes, Experiences, Reminders:

SESSION 31    Part C: Use **Medium** Sheet 1 from downloads
DATE:            Personal Notes, Experiences, Reminders:

SESSION 32    Part C: Use Medium Sheet 2 from downloads
DATE:            Personal Notes, Experiences, Reminders:

SESSION 33    Part C: Use Medium Sheet 3 from downloads
DATE:            Personal Notes, Experiences, Reminders:

SESSION 34    Part C: Use Medium Sheet 4 from downloads
DATE:        Personal Notes, Experiences, Reminders:

SESSION 35    Part C: Use Medium Sheet 5 from downloads
DATE:        Personal Notes, Experiences, Reminders:

SESSION 36    Part C: Use Medium Sheet 6 from downloads
DATE:        Personal Notes, Experiences, Reminders:

SESSION 37    Part C: Use Medium Sheet 7 from downloads
DATE:              Personal Notes, Experiences, Reminders:

SESSION 38    Part C: Use Medium Sheet 8 from downloads
DATE:              Personal Notes, Experiences, Reminders:

SESSION 39    Part C: Use Medium Sheet 9 from downloads
DATE:              Personal Notes, Experiences, Reminders:

SESSION 40    Part C: Use Medium Sheet 10 from downloads
DATE:         Personal Notes, Experiences, Reminders:




SESSION 41    Part C: Use Medium Sheet 11 from downloads
DATE:         Personal Notes, Experiences, Reminders:




SESSION 42    Part C: Use Medium Sheet 12 from downloads
DATE:         Personal Notes, Experiences, Reminders:

SESSION 43     Part C: Use Medium Sheet 13 from downloads
DATE:          Personal Notes, Experiences, Reminders:

SESSION 44     Part C: Use Medium Sheet 14 from downloads
DATE:          Personal Notes, Experiences, Reminders:

SESSION 45     Part C: Use Medium Sheet 15 from downloads
DATE:          Personal Notes, Experiences, Reminders:

SESSION 46    Part C: Use Medium Sheet 16 from downloads
DATE:          Personal Notes, Experiences, Reminders:

SESSION 47    Part C: Use Medium Sheet 17 from downloads
DATE:          Personal Notes, Experiences, Reminders:

SESSION 48    Part C: Use Medium Sheet 18 from downloads
DATE:          Personal Notes, Experiences, Reminders:

SESSION 49     Part C: Use Medium Sheet 19 from downloads
DATE:          Personal Notes, Experiences, Reminders:




SESSION 50     Part C: Use Medium Sheet 20 from downloads
DATE:          Personal Notes, Experiences, Reminders:




SESSION 51     Part C: Use Medium Sheet 21 from downloads
DATE:          Personal Notes, Experiences, Reminders:

SESSION 52    Part C: Use Medium Sheet 22 from downloads
DATE:         Personal Notes, Experiences, Reminders:

SESSION 53    Part C: Use **Small** Sheet 1 from downloads
DATE:         Personal Notes, Experiences, Reminders:

SESSION 54    Part C: Use Small Sheet 2 from downloads
DATE:         Personal Notes, Experiences, Reminders:

SESSION 55    Part C: Use Small Sheet 3 from downloads
DATE:            Personal Notes, Experiences, Reminders:

SESSION 56    Part C: Use Small Sheet 4 from downloads
DATE:            Personal Notes, Experiences, Reminders:

SESSION 57    Part C: Use Small Sheet 5 from downloads
DATE:            Personal Notes, Experiences, Reminders:

SESSION 58    Part C: Use Small Sheet 6 from downloads
DATE:              Personal Notes, Experiences, Reminders:




SESSION 59    Part C: Use Small Sheet 7 from downloads
DATE:              Personal Notes, Experiences, Reminders:




SESSION 60    Part C: Use Small Sheet 8 from downloads
DATE:              Personal Notes, Experiences, Reminders:

SESSION 61     Part C: Use Small Sheet 9 from downloads
DATE:          Personal Notes, Experiences, Reminders:

SESSION 62     Part C: Use Small Sheet 10 from downloads
DATE:          Personal Notes, Experiences, Reminders:

SESSION 63     Part C: Use Small Sheet 11 from downloads
DATE:          Personal Notes, Experiences, Reminders:

SESSION 64   Part C: Use Small Sheet 12 from downloads
DATE:        Personal Notes, Experiences, Reminders:

SESSION 65   Part C: Use Small Sheet 13 from downloads
DATE:        Personal Notes, Experiences, Reminders:

SESSION 66   Part C: Use Small Sheet 14 from downloads
DATE:        Personal Notes, Experiences, Reminders:

SESSION 67    Part C: Use Small Sheet 15 from downloads
DATE:          Personal Notes, Experiences, Reminders:

SESSION 68    Part C: Use Small Sheet 16 from downloads
DATE:          Personal Notes, Experiences, Reminders:

SESSION 69    Part C: Use Small Sheet 17 from downloads
DATE:          Personal Notes, Experiences, Reminders:

SESSION 70     Part C: Use Small Sheet 18 from downloads
DATE:          Personal Notes, Experiences, Reminders:

SESSION 71     Part C: Use Small Sheet 19 from downloads
DATE:          Personal Notes, Experiences, Reminders:

SESSION 72     Part C: Use Small Sheet 20 from downloads
DATE:          Personal Notes, Experiences, Reminders:

SESSION 73    Part C: Use Small Sheet 21 from downloads
DATE:         Personal Notes, Experiences, Reminders:

SESSION 74    Part C: Use Small Sheet 22 from downloads
DATE:         Personal Notes, Experiences, Reminders:

SESSION 75    Part C: Use Small Sheet 23 from downloads
DATE:         Personal Notes, Experiences, Reminders:

SESSION 76     Part C: Use Small Sheet 24 from downloads
DATE:          Personal Notes, Experiences, Reminders:

SESSION 77     Part C: Use Small Sheet 25 from downloads
DATE:          Personal Notes, Experiences, Reminders:

# Congratulations on Completing Phase 8

Incredible. Most people might not make it this far, but you did!

The Phase 8 survey will ask the following questions:

Was Phase 8 easier or more difficult than Phase 7?

Did you improve using your fingertip? Or did you improve any other way?

Do you have any suggestions for making Phase 8 better?

You can access the Phase 8 survey at
**www.learnmindsight.com/surveyphase8.html**

# PHASE 9 - CAPITAL LETTERS

You're ready to start reading letters! In Phase 9, you'll focus on capital letters.

**PHASE 9 HAS THREE PARTS: A, B, C**

Part A: Familiarization Using Your Eyes

Step 1: Print out the large capital letters from
**www.learnmindsight.com/phase9.html**

Step 2: At your own pace, for at least several days or weeks, work with one letter at a time. Instead of using a blindfold, you'll look at the letter with your eyes. Try to *feel* it as you look at it. Blink normally, of course. Then, close your eyes and see the letter with your mind. Don't be concerned about whether or not you're actually perceiving it or are using your memory.

Step 3: Also, work with using the palm of your hand, both touching the page and holding it just over the page. Feel the letter both ways while your eyes are open and looking at it as well as while keeping your eyes closed for a few minutes.

Step 4: Experiment with exposing the paper to your "windows" around your head and body. Do so with your eyes open as well as closed. Whenever your eyes are open, focus on your attention to your inner mental perception. For example, if you're holding the card behind your head, your open eyes won't help in any way, forcing you to rely solely on your mental perception while your eyes are open.

There are no journal entries for Part A since you'll decide how long to practice Part A on your own.

When you feel ready, continue to Part B.

Part B: Familiarization with Capital Letters

You will use the large capital letter cards from Part A. Just like Phase 1, Phase 9 Part B is entirely focused on familiarization. You will patiently train your mind to relate a card's impressions with a specific letter. You'll know when you're holding the letter Z, for example. As you work with it, you'll automatically train your brain to relate those impressions to "Z."

You'll also use differentiation to assist your learning process. Each session will use two letters. You'll learn about each letter partly by how distinct they feel from each other. Because of your previous work in Phases 5, 6, and 7, it's likely that you'll have strong visual impressions - that you'll _see_ the whole letter, or _part_ of the letter, directly.

SESSION LENGTH

Each Part B session is around an hour long. The first 20 minutes will be spent either listening to one of the online meditations, doing your own preparatory exercise, or simply relaxing while adjusting to wearing the blindfold. **The blindfold should be worn for the entire session.**

THREE ROUNDS OF ALTERNATING LETTERS AND RESTING BETWEEN THEM

Note: You can listen to a guided timer to use specifically for Part B. That way, you don't need to look at a timer to do this. Find the timer at **www.learnmindsight.com/phase9.html**

- Round 1: You'll work with the first letter for 5 minutes, then rest for 5 minutes, then repeat with the second letter.

- Round 2: You'll do the same, but instead of 5 minutes, each segment will last 4 minutes.

- Round 3: Same as above, but with segments lasting 3 minutes each.

As before, don't forget to include boredom busters when necessary.

## Part C: READING MEDIUM AND SMALL CAPITAL LETTERS[72]

### Step 1
Print out the <u>medium</u> and <u>small</u> capital letter sheets from
**www.learnmindsight.com/phase9.html**

### Step 2
Each print out has double-rows for each letter. That is to say, beneath each letter, you'll have space to draw the letter above it with glue. Phase 8 has a picture-example (using numbers).

You'll also be able to draw over the gray boundary lines between the letters with glue. The glue will need several hours to dry completely.

### Step 3
You'll work on one sheet per session, starting with Medium Capital Letters Sheet 1 (Session 28 in the journal below). Before working on a sheet, draw each letter using glue in the empty cell beneath the letter. This way, after working on a letter for a while, you can verify your impressions by touching the glue.

In the beginning, the sheets will be so simple that you'll remember what letters are on them, and this is good. You may even look at the sheet after it has dried, at the start of your session. This will help your brain relate to the impressions you'll receive after putting on your blindfold.

Work on each sheet for as long as it takes. Choose your preferred preparatory meditation or relaxation exercise to use before working on the sheet.

---

[72] I highly recommend you watch the month-long training videos on Wendy Gallant's YouTube channel in which Nikolay Denisov and Marina Kapirova trained her and Rob Freeman to read with fingers. Search YouTube using the term "Nikolay Denisov & Marina Teach Wendy Gallant, Rob Freeman"

SESSION 1          Part B: Use one "A" card and one "B" card
DATE:              Personal Notes, Experiences, Reminders:

SESSION 2          Part B: Use one "A" card and one "B" card
DATE:              Personal Notes, Experiences, Reminders:

SESSION 3          Part B: Use one "C" card and one "X" card
DATE:              Personal Notes, Experiences, Reminders:

SESSION 4    Part B: Use one "C" card and one "X" card
DATE:        Personal Notes, Experiences, Reminders:

SESSION 5    Part B: Use one "E" card and one "U" card
DATE:        Personal Notes, Experiences, Reminders:

SESSION 6    Part B: Use one "E" card and one "U" card
DATE:        Personal Notes, Experiences, Reminders:

SESSION 7        Part B: Use one "G" card and one "H" card
DATE:            Personal Notes, Experiences, Reminders:




SESSION 8        Part B: Use one "G" card and one "H" card
DATE:            Personal Notes, Experiences, Reminders:




SESSION 9        Part B: Use one "I" card and one "N" card
DATE:            Personal Notes, Experiences, Reminders:

SESSION 10    Part B: Use one "I" card and one "N" card
DATE:          Personal Notes, Experiences, Reminders:

SESSION 11    Part B: Use one "K" card and one "L" card
DATE:          Personal Notes, Experiences, Reminders:

SESSION 12    Part B: Use one "K" card and one "L" card
DATE:          Personal Notes, Experiences, Reminders:

SESSION 13     Part B: Use one "M" card and one "J" card
DATE:          Personal Notes, Experiences, Reminders:




SESSION 14     Part B: Use one "M" card and one "J" card
DATE:          Personal Notes, Experiences, Reminders:




SESSION 15     Part B: Use one "O" card and one "R" card
DATE:          Personal Notes, Experiences, Reminders:

SESSION 16     Part B: Use one "O" card and one "R" card
DATE:              Personal Notes, Experiences, Reminders:

SESSION 17     Part B: Use one "Q" card and one "P" card
DATE:              Personal Notes, Experiences, Reminders:

SESSION 18     Part B: Use one "Q" card and one "P" card
DATE:              Personal Notes, Experiences, Reminders:

SESSION 19     Part B: Use one "S" card and one "T" card
DATE:          Personal Notes, Experiences, Reminders:

SESSION 20     Part B: Use one "S" card and one "T" card
DATE:          Personal Notes, Experiences, Reminders:

SESSION 21     Part B: Use one "F" card and one "V" card
DATE:          Personal Notes, Experiences, Reminders:

SESSION 22　Part B: Use one "F" card and one "V" card
DATE:　　　Personal Notes, Experiences, Reminders:

SESSION 23　Part B: Use one "W" card and one "D" card
DATE:　　　Personal Notes, Experiences, Reminders:

SESSION 24　Part B: Use one "W" card and one "D" card
DATE:　　　Personal Notes, Experiences, Reminders:

SESSION 25  Part B: Use one "Y" card and one "Z" card
DATE:       Personal Notes, Experiences, Reminders:

SESSION 26  Part B: Use one "Y" card and one "Z" card
DATE:       Personal Notes, Experiences, Reminders:

SESSION 28  Part C: Use **Medium** Capital Letters Sheet 1
DATE:       Personal Notes, Experiences, Reminders:

SESSION 29    Part C: Use Medium Capital Letters Sheet 2
DATE:          Personal Notes, Experiences, Reminders:

SESSION 30    Part C: Use Medium Capital Letters Sheet 3
DATE:          Personal Notes, Experiences, Reminders:

SESSION 31    Part C: Use Medium Capital Letters Sheet 4
DATE:          Personal Notes, Experiences, Reminders:

SESSION 32    Part C: Use Medium Capital Letters Sheet 5
DATE:         Personal Notes, Experiences, Reminders:

SESSION 33    Part C: Use Medium Capital Letters Sheet 6
DATE:         Personal Notes, Experiences, Reminders:

SESSION 34    Part C: Use Medium Capital Letters Sheet 7
DATE:         Personal Notes, Experiences, Reminders:

SESSION 35     Part C: Use Medium Capital Letters Sheet 8
DATE:              Personal Notes, Experiences, Reminders:




SESSION 36     Part C: Use Medium Capital Letters Sheet 9
DATE:              Personal Notes, Experiences, Reminders:




SESSION 37     Part C: Use Medium Capital Letters Sheet 10
DATE:              Personal Notes, Experiences, Reminders:

SESSION 38    Part C: Use Medium Capital Letters Sheet 11
DATE:         Personal Notes, Experiences, Reminders:

SESSION 39    Part C: Use Medium Capital Letters Sheet 12
DATE:         Personal Notes, Experiences, Reminders:

SESSION 40    Part C: Use Medium Capital Letters Sheet 13
DATE:         Personal Notes, Experiences, Reminders:

SESSION 41    Part C: Use **Small** Capital Letters Sheet 1
DATE:          Personal Notes, Experiences, Reminders:

SESSION 42    Part C: Use Small Capital Letters Sheet 2
DATE:          Personal Notes, Experiences, Reminders:

SESSION 43    Part C: Use Small Capital Letters Sheet 3
DATE:          Personal Notes, Experiences, Reminders:

SESSION 44    Part C: Use Small Capital Letters Sheet 4
DATE:          Personal Notes, Experiences, Reminders:

SESSION 45    Part C: Use Small Capital Letters Sheet 5
DATE:          Personal Notes, Experiences, Reminders:

SESSION 46    Part C: Use Small Capital Letters Sheet 6
DATE:          Personal Notes, Experiences, Reminders:

SESSION 47    Part C: Use Small Capital Letters Sheet 7
DATE:         Personal Notes, Experiences, Reminders:




SESSION 48    Part C: Use Small Capital Letters Sheet 8
DATE:         Personal Notes, Experiences, Reminders:




SESSION 49    Part C: Use Small Capital Letters Sheet 9
DATE:         Personal Notes, Experiences, Reminders:

SESSION 50    Part C: Use Small Capital Letters Sheet 10
DATE:         Personal Notes, Experiences, Reminders:

SESSION 51    Part C: Use Small Capital Letters Sheet 11
DATE:         Personal Notes, Experiences, Reminders:

SESSION 52    Part C: Use Small Capital Letters Sheet 12
DATE:         Personal Notes, Experiences, Reminders:

SESSION 53    Part C: Use Small Capital Letters Sheet 13
DATE:          Personal Notes, Experiences, Reminders:

# Congratulations on Completing Phase 9

The Phase 9 survey will ask the following questions:

Was reading capital letters easier or more difficult than numbers? If so, why?

Did you improve using your fingertip? Or did you improve any other way?

How many days passed from your first Phase 9 session to your last? This will indicate how many days you rested or took off in between sessions.

Did you discover a way to improve Phase 9 to make it work better for you? And if so, what adjustments did you make?

You can access the Phase 9 survey at
**www.learnmindsight.com/surveyphase9.html**

# PHASE 10 - LOWER CASE LETTERS

You're ready to start reading lower case letters. You're getting closer to reading regular text found in books and magazines!

**PHASE 10 HAS THREE PARTS: A, B, C**

Part A: Familiarization Using Your Eyes

Step 1: Print out the large lower case letters from
**www.learnmindsight.com/phase10.html**

Step 2: At your own pace, for at least several days or weeks, work with one letter at a time. Instead of using a blindfold, you'll look at the letter with your eyes. Try to *feel* it as you look at it. Blink normally, of course. Then, close your eyes and see the letter with your mind. Don't be concerned about whether or not you're actually perceiving it or are using your memory.

Step 3: Also, work with using the palm of your hand, both touching the page and holding it just over the page. Feel the letter both ways while your eyes are open and looking at it as well as while keeping your eyes closed for a few minutes.

Step 4: Experiment with exposing the paper to your "windows" around your head and body. Do so with your eyes open as well as closed. Whenever your eyes are open, focus on your attention to your inner mental perception. For example, if you're holding the card behind your head, your open eyes won't help in any way, forcing you to rely solely on your mental perception while your eyes are open.

There are no journal entries for Part A since you'll decide how long to practice Part A on your own.

When you feel ready, continue to Part B.

## Part B: Familiarization with Lower Case Letters

You will use the cards from Part A. Just like Phase 1, Phase 10 Part B is entirely focused on familiarization. You will patiently train your mind to relate a card's impressions with a specific letter. You'll know when you're holding the letter y, for example. As you work with it, you'll automatically train your brain to relate those impressions to "y."

You'll also use differentiation to assist your learning process. Each session will use two letters. You'll learn about each letter partly by how distinct they feel from each other. Because of your previous work in Phases 5, 6, 7, and 9, it's likely that you'll have strong visual impressions - that you'll _see_ the whole letter, or _part_ of the letter, directly.

SESSION LENGTH
Each Part B session is around an hour long. The first 20 minutes will be spent either listening to one of the online meditations, doing your own preparatory exercise, or simply relaxing while adjusting to wearing the blindfold. **The blindfold should be worn for the entire session.**

THREE ROUNDS OF ALTERNATING LETTERS AND RESTING BETWEEN THEM
Note: You can listen to a guided timer to use specifically for Part B. That way, you don't need to look at a timer to do this. Find the timer at
**www.learnmindsight.com/phase10.html**

- Round 1: You'll work with the first letter for 5 minutes, then rest for 5 minutes, then repeat with the second letter.

- Round 2: You'll do the same, but instead of 5 minutes, each segment will last 4 minutes.

- Round 3: Same as above, but with segments lasting 3 minutes each.

As before, don't forget to include boredom busters when necessary.

## Part C: READING MEDIUM AND SMALL LOWER CASE LETTERS

<u>Step 1</u>
Print out the <u>medium</u> and <u>small</u> lower case sheets from
**www.learnmindsight.com/phase10.html**

<u>Step 2</u>
Each print out has double-rows of letters, just like Phase 8 and 9. That is to say, beneath each letter, you'll have space to draw the letter above it with glue.

You'll also be able to draw over the gray boundary lines between the letters with glue. The glue will need several hours to dry completely.

<u>Step 3</u>
You'll work on one sheet per session, starting with Medium Lower Case Letters Sheet 1 (Session 28 in the journal below). Before working on a sheet, draw each letter using glue in the empty cell beneath the letter. This way, after working on a letter for a while, you can verify your impressions by touching the glue.

In the beginning, the sheets will be so simple that you'll remember what letters are on them, and this is good. You may even look at the sheet after it has dried, at the start of your session. This will help your brain relate to the impressions you'll receive after putting on your blindfold.

Work on each sheet for as long as it takes. Choose your preferred preparatory meditation or relaxation exercise to use before working on the sheet.

SESSION 1          Part B: Use one "a" card and one "b" card
DATE:              Personal Notes, Experiences, Reminders:

SESSION 2          Part B: Use one "a" card and one "b" card
DATE:              Personal Notes, Experiences, Reminders:

SESSION 3          Part B: Use one "c" card and one "x" card
DATE:              Personal Notes, Experiences, Reminders:

SESSION 4  Part B: Use one "c" card and one "x" card
DATE:      Personal Notes, Experiences, Reminders:

SESSION 5  Part B: Use one "e" card and one "u" card
DATE:      Personal Notes, Experiences, Reminders:

SESSION 6  Part B: Use one "e" card and one "u" card
DATE:      Personal Notes, Experiences, Reminders:

SESSION 7    Part B: Use one "g" card and one "h" card
DATE:        Personal Notes, Experiences, Reminders:

SESSION 8    Part B: Use one "g" card and one "h" card
DATE:        Personal Notes, Experiences, Reminders:

SESSION 9    Part B: Use one "i" card and one "n" card
DATE:        Personal Notes, Experiences, Reminders:

SESSION 10    Part B: Use one "i" card and one "n" card
DATE:         Personal Notes, Experiences, Reminders:

SESSION 11    Part B: Use one "k" card and one "l (L)" card
DATE:         Personal Notes, Experiences, Reminders:

SESSION 12    Part B: Use one "k" card and one "l" card
DATE:         Personal Notes, Experiences, Reminders:

SESSION 13    Part B: Use one "m" card and one "j" card
DATE:         Personal Notes, Experiences, Reminders:

SESSION 14    Part B: Use one "m" card and one "j" card
DATE:         Personal Notes, Experiences, Reminders:

SESSION 15    Part B: Use one "o" card and one "r" card
DATE:         Personal Notes, Experiences, Reminders:

SESSION 16     Part B: Use one "o" card and one "r" card
DATE:          Personal Notes, Experiences, Reminders:

SESSION 17     Part B: Use one "q" card and one "s" card
DATE:          Personal Notes, Experiences, Reminders:

SESSION 18     Part B: Use one "q" card and one "s" card
DATE:          Personal Notes, Experiences, Reminders:

SESSION 19    Part B: Use one "p" card and one "t" card
DATE:         Personal Notes, Experiences, Reminders:




SESSION 20    Part B: Use one "p" card and one "t" card
DATE:         Personal Notes, Experiences, Reminders:




SESSION 21    Part B: Use one "f" card and one "v" card
DATE:         Personal Notes, Experiences, Reminders:

SESSION 22    Part B: Use one "f" card and one "v" card
DATE:         Personal Notes, Experiences, Reminders:

SESSION 23    Part B: Use one "w" card and one "d" card
DATE:         Personal Notes, Experiences, Reminders:

SESSION 24    Part B: Use one "w" card and one "d" card
DATE:         Personal Notes, Experiences, Reminders:

SESSION 25    Part B: Use one "y" card and one "z" card
DATE:             Personal Notes, Experiences, Reminders:

SESSION 26    Part B: Use one "y" card and one "z" card
DATE:             Personal Notes, Experiences, Reminders:

SESSION 28    Part C: Use **Medium** Lower Case Letters Sheet 1
DATE:             Personal Notes, Experiences, Reminders:

SESSION 29    Part C: Use Medium Lower Case Letters Sheet 2
DATE:        Personal Notes, Experiences, Reminders:

SESSION 30    Part C: Use Medium Lower Case Letters Sheet 3
DATE:        Personal Notes, Experiences, Reminders:

SESSION 31    Part C: Use Medium Lower Case Letters Sheet 4
DATE:        Personal Notes, Experiences, Reminders:

SESSION 32    Part C: Use Medium Lower Case Letters Sheet 5
DATE:         Personal Notes, Experiences, Reminders:

SESSION 33    Part C: Use Medium Lower Case Letters Sheet 6
DATE:         Personal Notes, Experiences, Reminders:

SESSION 34    Part C: Use Medium Lower Case Letters Sheet 7
DATE:         Personal Notes, Experiences, Reminders:

SESSION 35    Part C: Use Medium Lower Case Letters Sheet 8
DATE:         Personal Notes, Experiences, Reminders:

SESSION 36    Part C: Use Medium Lower Case Letters Sheet 9
DATE:         Personal Notes, Experiences, Reminders:

SESSION 37    Part C: Use Medium Lower Case Letters Sheet 10
DATE:         Personal Notes, Experiences, Reminders:

SESSION 38     Part C: Use Medium Lower Case Letters Sheet 11
DATE:          Personal Notes, Experiences, Reminders:

SESSION 39     Part C: Use Medium Lower Case Letters Sheet 12
DATE:          Personal Notes, Experiences, Reminders:

SESSION 40     Part C: Use Medium Lower Case Letters Sheet 13
DATE:          Personal Notes, Experiences, Reminders:

SESSION 41   Part C: Use **Small** Lower Case Letters Sheet 1
DATE:        Personal Notes, Experiences, Reminders:

SESSION 42   Part C: Use Small Lower Case Letters Sheet 2
DATE:        Personal Notes, Experiences, Reminders:

SESSION 43   Part C: Use Small Lower Case Letters Sheet 3
DATE:        Personal Notes, Experiences, Reminders:

SESSION 44    Part C: Use Small Lower Case Letters Sheet 4
DATE:         Personal Notes, Experiences, Reminders:

SESSION 45    Part C: Use Small Lower Case Letters Sheet 5
DATE:         Personal Notes, Experiences, Reminders:

SESSION 46    Part C: Use Small Lower Case Letters Sheet 6
DATE:         Personal Notes, Experiences, Reminders:

SESSION 47    Part C: Use Small Lower Case Letters Sheet 7
DATE:         Personal Notes, Experiences, Reminders:

SESSION 48    Part C: Use Small Lower Case Letters Sheet 8
DATE:         Personal Notes, Experiences, Reminders:

SESSION 49    Part C: Use Small Lower Case Letters Sheet 9
DATE:         Personal Notes, Experiences, Reminders:

SESSION 50    Part C: Use Small Lower Case Letters 10
DATE:               Personal Notes, Experiences, Reminders:

SESSION 51    Part C: Use Small Lower Case Letters Sheet 11
DATE:               Personal Notes, Experiences, Reminders:

SESSION 52    Part C: Use Small Lower Case Letters Sheet 12
DATE:               Personal Notes, Experiences, Reminders:

SESSION 53    Part C: Use Small Lower Case Letters Sheet 13
DATE:          Personal Notes, Experiences, Reminders:

# Congratulations on Completing Phase 10

The Phase 10 survey will ask the following questions:

When you were done, did you feel you needed more sheets to practice with, or was this a good amount?

Was reading lower case letters easier or more difficult than capital letters? If so, why?

Did you improve using your fingertip? Or did you improve any other way?

How many days passed from your first Phase 10 session to your last? This will indicate how many days you rested or took off in between sessions.

Did you discover a way to improve Phase 10 to make it work better for you? And if so, what adjustments did you make?

You can access the Phase 10 survey at
**www.learnmindsight.com/surveyphase10.html**

# PHASE 11 - UPPER & LOWER CASE COUNTERPARTS

In Phase 11, you'll work with two letters at a time. They are the same letter. On each "counterparts letters" sheet, the upper-case letter is to the left, and next to it, its lower-case counterpart. This phase is brief compared to the previous ones because it assumes you succeeded at perceiving capital letters in Phase 9 and lower case letters in Phase 10.

Step 1: Print out the medium and small counterparts sheets (we don't use large cards/letters in Phase 11) from **www.learnmindsight.com/phase11.html**

Step 2: These sheets are just like those in Phases 9 and 10, and are also meant for using glue. Don't be concerned with using the glue to draw both the upper case and lower case version of the letter, pick either one in the interest of time and space.

Work on each sheet for as long as it takes. Choose your preferred preparatory meditation or relaxation exercise to use before working on the sheet.

SESSION 1     Use **Medium** Counterparts Letters Sheet 1
DATE:         Personal Notes, Experiences, Reminders:

SESSION 2     Use Medium Counterparts Letters Sheet 2
DATE:         Personal Notes, Experiences, Reminders:

SESSION 3     Use Medium Counterparts Letters Sheet 3
DATE:         Personal Notes, Experiences, Reminders:

SESSION 4    Use Medium Counterparts Letters Sheet 4
DATE:        Personal Notes, Experiences, Reminders:

SESSION 5    Use Medium Counterparts Letters Sheet 5
DATE:        Personal Notes, Experiences, Reminders:

SESSION 6    Use Medium Counterparts Letters Sheet 6
DATE:        Personal Notes, Experiences, Reminders:

SESSION 7     Use Medium Counterparts Letters Sheet 7
DATE:        Personal Notes, Experiences, Reminders:

SESSION 8     Use Medium Counterparts Letters Sheet 8
DATE:        Personal Notes, Experiences, Reminders:

SESSION 9     Use Medium Counterparts Letters Sheet 9
DATE:        Personal Notes, Experiences, Reminders:

SESSION 10    Use Medium Counterparts Letters Sheet 10
DATE:         Personal Notes, Experiences, Reminders:

SESSION 11    Use Medium Counterparts Letters Sheet 11
DATE:         Personal Notes, Experiences, Reminders:

SESSION 12    Use Medium Counterparts Letters Sheet 12
DATE:         Personal Notes, Experiences, Reminders:

SESSION 13    Use Medium Counterparts Letters Sheet 13
DATE:         Personal Notes, Experiences, Reminders:

SESSION 14    Use Medium Counterparts Letters Sheet 14
DATE:         Personal Notes, Experiences, Reminders:

SESSION 15    Use Medium Counterparts Letters Sheet 15
DATE:         Personal Notes, Experiences, Reminders:

SESSION 16   Use Medium Counterparts Letters Sheet 16
DATE:        Personal Notes, Experiences, Reminders:

SESSION 17   Use Medium Counterparts Letters Sheet 17
DATE:        Personal Notes, Experiences, Reminders:

SESSION 18   Use Medium Counterparts Letters Sheet 18
DATE:        Personal Notes, Experiences, Reminders:

SESSION 19     Use Medium Counterparts Letters Sheet 19
DATE:          Personal Notes, Experiences, Reminders:

SESSION 20     Use Medium Counterparts Letters Sheet 20
DATE:          Personal Notes, Experiences, Reminders:

SESSION 21     Use **Small** Counterparts Letters Sheet 1
DATE:          Personal Notes, Experiences, Reminders:

SESSION 22    Use Small Counterparts Letters Sheet 2
DATE:         Personal Notes, Experiences, Reminders:




SESSION 23    Use Small Counterparts Letters Sheet 3
DATE:         Personal Notes, Experiences, Reminders:




SESSION 24    Use Small Counterparts Letters Sheet 4
DATE:         Personal Notes, Experiences, Reminders:

SESSION 25    Use Small Counterparts Letters Sheet 5
DATE:         Personal Notes, Experiences, Reminders:

SESSION 26    Use Small Counterparts Letters Sheet 6
DATE:         Personal Notes, Experiences, Reminders:

SESSION 27    Use Small Counterparts Letters Sheet 7
DATE:         Personal Notes, Experiences, Reminders:

SESSION 28    Use Small Counterparts Letters Sheet 8
DATE:          Personal Notes, Experiences, Reminders:

SESSION 29    Use Small Counterparts Letters Sheet 9
DATE:          Personal Notes, Experiences, Reminders:

SESSION 30    Use Small Counterparts Letters Sheet 10
DATE:          Personal Notes, Experiences, Reminders:

SESSION 31     Use Small Counterparts Letters Sheet 11
DATE:          Personal Notes, Experiences, Reminders:

SESSION 32     Use Small Counterparts Letters Sheet 12
DATE:          Personal Notes, Experiences, Reminders:

SESSION 33     Use Small Counterparts Letters Sheet 13
DATE:          Personal Notes, Experiences, Reminders:

SESSION 34    Use Small Counterparts Letters Sheet 14
DATE:         Personal Notes, Experiences, Reminders:

SESSION 35    Use Small Counterparts Letters Sheet 15
DATE:         Personal Notes, Experiences, Reminders:

SESSION 36    Use Small Counterparts Letters Sheet 16
DATE:         Personal Notes, Experiences, Reminders:

SESSION 37    Use Small Counterparts Letters Sheet 17
DATE:         Personal Notes, Experiences, Reminders:

SESSION 38    Use Small Counterparts Letters Sheet 18
DATE:         Personal Notes, Experiences, Reminders:

SESSION 39    Use Small Counterparts Letters Sheet 19
DATE:         Personal Notes, Experiences, Reminders:

SESSION 40    Use Small Counterparts Letters Sheet 20
DATE:         Personal Notes, Experiences, Reminders:

# Congratulations on Completing Phase 11

The Phase 11 survey will ask the following questions:

When you were done, did you feel you needed more sheets to practice with, or was this a good amount?

Was it helpful and/or challenging to perceive a capital letter next to its lower-case counterpart?

How many days passed from your first Phase 11 session to your last? This will indicate how many days you rested or took off in between sessions.

Did you discover a way to improve Phase 11 to make it work better for you? And if so, what adjustments did you make?

You can access the Phase 11 survey at
**www.learnmindsight.com/surveyphase11.html**

# PHASE 12 - UPPER CASE WORDS

Now, you'll work with two letter and three letter words where all the letters are capitalized.

<u>There are four parts to Phase 12</u>
PART A: Familiarization with two letter words

PART B: Using the two letter "mixed-size" sheets for <u>upper</u> case words

PART C: Familiarization with three letter words

Part D: Using the three letter "mixed-size" sheets for <u>upper</u> case words

<u>PART A</u>

Step 1: Print out the <u>large cap two letter words</u> from **www.learnmindsight.com/phase12.html**

Step 2: At your own pace, for at least several days or weeks, work with as many words as you like during each session. Instead of using a blindfold, you'll look at the word with your eyes. Try to *feel* it as you look at it. Blink normally, of course. Then, close your eyes and see the word with your mind. Don't be concerned about whether or not you're actually perceiving it or are using your memory.

Step 3: Also, work with using the palm of your hand, both touching the page and holding it just over the page. Feel the word both ways while your eyes are open and looking at it as well as while keeping your eyes closed for a few minutes.

Step 4: Experiment with exposing the paper to your "windows" around your head and body. Do so with your eyes open as well as closed. Whenever your eyes are open, focus on your attention to your inner mental perception. For example, if you're holding the card behind your head, your open eyes won't help in any way, forcing you to rely solely on your mental perception while your eyes are open.
<u>There are no journal entries</u> for Part A or Part C since you'll decide how long to practice them on your own.

When you feel ready, continue to Part B.

## Part B: READING TWO LETTER WORDS

Step 1
Print out the <u>capital two letter mixed size</u> sheets from
**www.learnmindsight.com/phase12.html**

Step 2
Each print out has double-rows for each word. That is to say, beneath each word, you'll have space to draw the word above it with glue. Phase 8 has a picture-example (using numbers).

You'll also be able to draw over the gray boundary lines between the words with glue. The glue will need several hours to dry completely.

Step 3
You'll work on one sheet per session, starting with Capital 2 Letter Mixed Size Sheet 1. Before working on a sheet, draw each word using glue in the empty cell beneath the letter. This way, after working on a word for a while, you can verify your impressions by touching the glue.

## PART C: FAMILIARIZATION WITH THREE LETTER WORDS

Part C is exactly like Part A except now it's with <u>three letter</u> words. Print out the <u>large cap three letter words</u> from
**www.learnmindsight.com/phase12.html**

Remember, there's **no journaling below for Part C (or A)** since you'll determine how long you want to spend before beginning Parts B and D.

## PART D: READING THREE LETTER WORDS

Part D is exactly like Part B except now it's with <u>three letter</u> words.  Print out the <u>capital three letter mixed size</u> sheets from
**www.learnmindsight.com/phase12.html**

SESSION 1          Part B: Use Capital **Two** Letter Mixed Size Sheet 1
DATE:              Personal Notes, Experiences, Reminders:




SESSION 2          Part B: Use Capital Two Letter Mixed Size Sheet 2
DATE:              Personal Notes, Experiences, Reminders:




SESSION 3          Part B: Use Capital Two Letter Mixed Size Sheet 3
DATE:              Personal Notes, Experiences, Reminders:

SESSION 4    Part B: Use Capital Two Letter Mixed Size Sheet 4
DATE:         Personal Notes, Experiences, Reminders:




SESSION 5    Part B: Use Capital Two Letter Mixed Size Sheet 5
DATE:         Personal Notes, Experiences, Reminders:




SESSION 6    Part B: Use Capital Two Letter Mixed Size Sheet 6
DATE:         Personal Notes, Experiences, Reminders:

SESSION 7    Part D: Use Capital **Three Letter** Mixed Size Sheet 1
DATE:        Personal Notes, Experiences, Reminders:

SESSION 8    Part D: Use Capital Three Letter Mixed Size Sheet 2
DATE:        Personal Notes, Experiences, Reminders:

SESSION 9    Part D: Use Capital Three Letter Mixed Size Sheet 3
DATE:        Personal Notes, Experiences, Reminders:

SESSION 10    Part D: Use Capital Three Letter Mixed Size Sheet 4
DATE:          Personal Notes, Experiences, Reminders:

SESSION 11    Part D: Use Capital Three Letter Mixed Size Sheet 5
DATE:          Personal Notes, Experiences, Reminders:

SESSION 12    Part D: Use Capital Three Letter Mixed Size Sheet 6
DATE:          Personal Notes, Experiences, Reminders:

SESSION 13    Part D: Use Capital Three Letter Mixed Size Sheet 7
DATE:         Personal Notes, Experiences, Reminders:

SESSION 14    Part D: Use Capital Three Letter Mixed Size Sheet 8
DATE:         Personal Notes, Experiences, Reminders:

SESSION 15    Part D: Use Capital Three Letter Mixed Size Sheet 9
DATE:         Personal Notes, Experiences, Reminders:

SESSION 16     Part D: Use Capital Three Letter Mixed Size Sheet 10
DATE:          Personal Notes, Experiences, Reminders:

SESSION 17     Part D: Use Capital Three Letter Mixed Size Sheet 11
DATE:          Personal Notes, Experiences, Reminders:

SESSION 18     Part D: Use Capital Three Letter Mixed Size Sheet 12
DATE:          Personal Notes, Experiences, Reminders:

SESSION 19    Part D: Use Capital Three Letter Mixed Size Sheet 13
DATE:             Personal Notes, Experiences, Reminders:

SESSION 20    Part D: Use Capital Three Letter Mixed Size Sheet 14
DATE:             Personal Notes, Experiences, Reminders:

SESSION 21    Part D: Use Capital Three Letter Mixed Size Sheet 15
DATE:             Personal Notes, Experiences, Reminders:

SESSION 22    Part D: Use Capital Three Letter Mixed Size Sheet 16
DATE:         Personal Notes, Experiences, Reminders:




SESSION 23    Part D: Use Capital Three Letter Mixed Size Sheet 17
DATE:         Personal Notes, Experiences, Reminders:




SESSION 24    Part D: Use Capital Three Letter Mixed Size Sheet 18
DATE:         Personal Notes, Experiences, Reminders:

# Congratulations on Completing Phase 12

Look how far you've come! As I write this section of the book, I truly wonder how many people will make it this far. If you're one of them, I want to thank you for all the hard work you've put in. We have so much to learn about how our world operates, including our bodies and minds.

The Phase 12 survey will ask the following questions:

When you were done, did you feel you needed more sheets to practice with, or was this a good amount?

Was there much difference in how challenging working with three letter words was compared to two letter words? Or was it about the same?

How long did you spend on Parts A and C (the large printouts of the words)? Or, did you skip them, and go straight to Parts B and D?

How many days passed from your first Phase 12 session to your last?

Did you discover a way to improve Phase 12 to make it work better for you? And if so, what adjustments did you make?

You can access the Phase 12 survey at
**www.learnmindsight.com/surveyphase12.html**

# PHASE 13 - LOWER CASE WORDS

Now, you'll work with two letter and three letter words where all the letters are in lower-case. Phase 13 is exactly like Phase 12.

There are four parts to Phase 13
PART A: Familiarization with two letter words

PART B: Using the two letter "mixed-size" sheets for lower case words

PART C: Familiarization with three letter words

Part D: Using the three letter "mixed-size" sheets for lower case words

PART A

Step 1: Print out the large lower case two Letter words from
**www.learnmindsight.com/phase13.html**

Step 2: At your own pace, for at least several days or weeks, work with as many words as you like during each session. Instead of using a blindfold, you'll look at the word with your eyes. Try to *feel* it as you look at it. Blink normally, of course. Then, close your eyes and see the word with your mind. Don't be concerned about whether or not you're actually perceiving it or are using your memory.

Step 3: Also, work with using the palm of your hand, both touching the page and holding it just over the page. Feel the word both ways while your eyes are open and looking at it as well as while keeping your eyes closed for a few minutes.

Step 4: Experiment with exposing the paper to your "windows" around your head and body. Do so with your eyes open as well as closed. Whenever your eyes are open, focus on your attention to your inner mental perception. For example, if you're holding the card behind your head, your open eyes won't help in any way, forcing you to rely solely on your mental perception while your eyes are open. There are no journal entries for Part A or Part C since you'll decide how long to practice them on your own.

When you feel ready, continue to Part B.

## Part B: READING TWO LETTER WORDS

### Step 1
Print out the <u>lower case two letter mixed size</u> sheets from
**www.learnmindsight.com/phase13.html**

### Step 2
Each print out has double-rows for each word. That is to say, beneath each word, you'll have space to draw the word above it with glue. Phase 8 has a picture-example using numbers instead of letters or words.

You'll also be able to draw over the gray boundary lines between the words with glue. The glue will need several hours to dry completely.

### Step 3
You'll work on one sheet per session, starting with Lower Case 2 Letter Mixed Size Sheet 1. Before working on a sheet, draw each word using glue in the empty cell beneath the letter. This way, after working on a word for a while, you can verify your impressions by touching the glue.

## PART C: FAMILIARIZATION WITH **THREE** LETTER WORDS

Part C is exactly like Part A except now it's with <u>three letter</u> words. Print out the <u>large lower case three letter words</u> from
**www.learnmindsight.com/phase13.html**

Remember, there's **no journaling below for Part C (or A)** since you'll determine how long you want to spend before beginning Parts B and D.

## PART D: READING THREE LETTER WORDS

Part D is exactly like Part B except now it's with <u>three letter</u> words. Print out the <u>lower case three letter mixed size</u> sheets from
**www.learnmindsight.com/phase13.html**

SESSION 1     Part B: Lower Case **Two** Letter Mixed Size Sheet 1
DATE:         Personal Notes, Experiences, Reminders:

SESSION 2     Part B: Lower Case Two Letter Mixed Size Sheet 2
DATE:         Personal Notes, Experiences, Reminders:

SESSION 3     Part B: Lower Case Two Letter Mixed Size Sheet 3
DATE:         Personal Notes, Experiences, Reminders:

SESSION 4      Part B: Lower Case Two Letter Mixed Size Sheet 4
DATE:          Personal Notes, Experiences, Reminders:

SESSION 5      Part B: Lower Case Two Letter Mixed Size Sheet 5
DATE:          Personal Notes, Experiences, Reminders:

SESSION 6      Part B: Lower Case Two Letter Mixed Size Sheet 6
DATE:          Personal Notes, Experiences, Reminders:

SESSION 7    Part C: Lower Case **Three** Letter Mixed Size Sheet 1
DATE:        Personal Notes, Experiences, Reminders:




SESSION 8    Part C: Use Capital Three Letter Mixed Size Sheet 2
DATE:        Personal Notes, Experiences, Reminders:




SESSION 9    Part C: Use Capital Three Letter Mixed Size Sheet 3
DATE:        Personal Notes, Experiences, Reminders:

SESSION 10    Part B: Use Capital Three Letter Mixed Size Sheet 4
DATE:         Personal Notes, Experiences, Reminders:

SESSION 11    Part C: Use Capital Three Letter Mixed Size Sheet 5
DATE:         Personal Notes, Experiences, Reminders:

SESSION 12    Part C: Use Capital Three Letter Mixed Size Sheet 6
DATE:         Personal Notes, Experiences, Reminders:

SESSION 13     Part B: Use Capital Three Letter Mixed Size Sheet 7
DATE:          Personal Notes, Experiences, Reminders:

SESSION 14     Part C: Use Capital Three Letter Mixed Size Sheet 8
DATE:          Personal Notes, Experiences, Reminders:

SESSION 15     Part C: Use Capital Three Letter Mixed Size Sheet 9
DATE:          Personal Notes, Experiences, Reminders:

SESSION 16     Part B: Use Capital Three Letter Mixed Size Sheet 10
DATE:          Personal Notes, Experiences, Reminders:

SESSION 17     Part C: Use Capital Three Letter Mixed Size Sheet 11
DATE:          Personal Notes, Experiences, Reminders:

SESSION 18     Part C: Use Capital Three Letter Mixed Size Sheet 12
DATE:          Personal Notes, Experiences, Reminders:

SESSION 19    Part C: Use Capital Three Letter Mixed Size Sheet 13
DATE:        Personal Notes, Experiences, Reminders:

SESSION 20    Part C: Use Capital Three Letter Mixed Size Sheet 14
DATE:        Personal Notes, Experiences, Reminders:

SESSION 21    Part C: Use Capital Three Letter Mixed Size Sheet 15
DATE:        Personal Notes, Experiences, Reminders:

SESSION 22    Part C: Use Capital Three Letter Mixed Size Sheet 16
DATE:        Personal Notes, Experiences, Reminders:

# Congratulations on Completing Phase 13

The Phase 13 survey will ask the following questions:

When you were done, did you feel you needed more sheets to practice with, or was this a good amount?

Was there much difference between working with lower case words (Phase 13) and capitalized words (Phase 12)? Or was it about the same?

How long did you spend on Parts A and C (the large printouts of the words)? Or, did you skip them, and go straight to Parts B and D?

How many days passed from your first Phase 13 session to your last?

Did you discover a way to improve Phase 13 to make it work better for you? And if so, what adjustments did you make?

You can access the Phase 13 survey at
**www.learnmindsight.com/surveyphase13.html**

# PHASE 14 - CAPITALIZED WORDS

Now, you'll work with four letter words, whose first letter will be capitalized and the rest lower case. Phase 14 is similar to Phase 13.

There are two parts to Phase 14, Part A and Part B

PART A: Familiarization with four letter words

Step 1: Print out the large four letter words from
**www.learnmindsight.com/phase14.html**

Step 2: At your own pace, for at least several days or weeks, work with as many words as you like during each session. Instead of using a blindfold, you'll look at the word with your eyes. Try to *feel* it as you look at it. Blink normally, of course. Then, close your eyes and see the word with your mind. Don't be concerned about whether or not you're actually perceiving it or are using your memory.

Step 3: Also, work with using the palm of your hand, both touching the page and holding it just over the page. Feel the word both ways while your eyes are open and looking at it as well as while keeping your eyes closed for a few minutes.

Step 4: Experiment with exposing the paper to your "windows" around your head and body. Do so with your eyes open as well as closed. Whenever your eyes are open, focus on your attention to your inner mental perception. For example, if you're holding the card behind your head, your open eyes won't help in any way, forcing you to rely solely on your mental perception while your eyes are open.

There are no journal entries for Part A since you'll decide how long to practice them on your own.

When you feel ready, continue to Part B.

Part B: READING FOUR LETTER WORDS

Step 1
Print out the four letter word sheets from
**www.learnmindsight.com/phase14.html**

Step 2
Each print out has double-rows for each word. That is to say, beneath each word, you'll have space to draw the word above it with glue. Phase 8 has a picture-example (using numbers).

You'll also be able to draw over the gray boundary lines between the words with glue. The glue will need several hours to dry completely.

** Because of the length of the words in this phase, using glue is more difficult due to lack of space. You might draw only under the large font word, knowing the smaller font word next to it is the same word.

Step 3
You'll work on one sheet per session, starting with "four letter word sheet 1." Before working on a sheet, draw each word using glue in the empty cell beneath the letter. This way, after working on a word for a while, you can verify your impressions by touching the glue.

**Don't forget you can still use the "fingertip" instruction from Phase 8.**

SESSION 1      Part B: Four Letter Word Sheet 1
DATE:          Personal Notes, Experiences, Reminders:

SESSION 2      Part B: Four Letter Word Sheet 2
DATE:          Personal Notes, Experiences, Reminders:

SESSION 3      Part B: Four Letter Word Sheet 3
DATE:          Personal Notes, Experiences, Reminders:

SESSION 4      Part B: Four Letter Word Sheet 4
DATE:             Personal Notes, Experiences, Reminders:




SESSION 5      Part B: Four Letter Word Sheet 5
DATE:             Personal Notes, Experiences, Reminders:




SESSION 6      Part B: Four Letter Word Sheet 6
DATE:             Personal Notes, Experiences, Reminders:

SESSION 7    Part B: Four Letter Word Sheet 7
DATE:       Personal Notes, Experiences, Reminders:

SESSION 8    Part B: Four Letter Word Sheet 8
DATE:       Personal Notes, Experiences, Reminders:

SESSION 9    Part B: Four Letter Word Sheet 9
DATE:       Personal Notes, Experiences, Reminders:

SESSION 10    Part B: Four Letter Word Sheet 10
DATE:         Personal Notes, Experiences, Reminders:

SESSION 11    Part B: Four Letter Word Sheet 11
DATE:         Personal Notes, Experiences, Reminders:

SESSION 12    Part B: Four Letter Word Sheet 12
DATE:         Personal Notes, Experiences, Reminders:

# Congratulations on Completing Phase 14

You have completed the entire pilot program. The word "congratulations" doesn't do your accomplishment justice. If you've taken it step-by-step, moving on to the next phase only after succeeding at the previous one, then your consciousness has grown in ways few people understand. It surpasses language. I hope you still have enough energy left to complete one final survey.

When you were done, did you feel you needed more sheets to practice with, or was this a good amount?

Was there much difference between working with Phase 14 words and those of Phases 12 and 13?

How long did you spend on Parts A (the large printouts of the words)? Or, did you skip them, and go straight to Parts B?

How many days passed from your first Phase 14 session to your last?

Did you discover a way to improve Phase 14 to make it work better for you? And if so, what adjustments did you make?

What benefits did you experience from this training over all this time, aside from increasing your perceptual sensitivity? How did it change you?

You can access the Phase 14 survey at
**www.learnmindsight.com/surveyphase14.html**

# NEXT STEPS

If you completed every phase successfully, then you'll undoubtedly feel confident about your ability to learn new skills. This reflects your "growth mindset." Also, you trained yourself, which is important. You figured out how to work with your mind to give you what you've been searching for.

You can continue teaching yourself. It's easy, simply pick up a newspaper and start reading. Even though I included instructions for using glue in each phase, I wouldn't be surprised if some of you stopped using glue sometime before the final phases. The glue is like a bicycle's training wheels. After a while, they're unnecessary and even hold you back.

You might also explore children's books with pictures inside. You can see colors, and hopefully, their boundaries. That's all that pictures are, colors with boundaries. Playing cards are a popular option too.

You might also revisit Part 2, "Across Space and Time," and experiment with the psychic side of Mind Sight.

Taking it further, you could read the entry from the *Journal of Scientific Exploration*[73] about the children who combined seeing without eyes with psychokinesis and teleportation. You're basically at their level. The journal has general instructions for recreating their experiments.

You could also find positive, helpful applications for Mind Sight. You have the potential to become an effective energy healer. See yourself perceiving someone's physical or energetic state to understand their illness and discomfort. Imagine if you could intuit how to best support their journey toward healing while preserving their autonomy. Formal training in energy work will be important.

This is my way of wishing you the best. This skill is yours to do with as you want. Please don't infringe on others' right to thrive and prosper.

If you train children in this ability, protect them. Please don't force them into the limelight or a laboratory. Similar advice may benefit you as well. You're more likely to have a long and healthy relationship with these abilities if you keep them relatively private.

Hopefully, now you see that achieving Mind Sight wasn't the most important part of this program. It was everything you learned about yourself along the way that mattered. I wish you much happiness.

---

[73] Shen, Dong. (2010). Unexpected Behavior of Matter in Conjunction with Human Consciousness. *Journal of Scientific Exploration*. Volume 24(1). https://www.scientificexploration.org/journal/volume-24-number-1-2010

# RECOMMENDED READING

Hopkins, Lloyd F. (1988). *Mind Sight and Perception*. Valley Press.

Romains, Jules. (1978). *Eyeless Sight*. Citadel Press.

Eagleman, David. (2017). *The Brain: The Story of You*. Vintage.

Ostrander, S., & Schroeder, L. (1970). *Psychic Discoveries Behind the Iron Curtain*. Prentice Hall.

Radin Ph.D., Dean. (2018). *Real Magic: Ancient Wisdom, Modern Science, and a Guide to the Secret Power of the Universe*. Harmony.

Ring Ph.D., Kenneth. (2008). *Mindsight: Near-Death and Out-of-Body Experiences in the Blind*. iUniverse.

Alexander M.D., Eben. (2012). *Proof of Heaven: A Neurosurgeon's Journey into the Afterlife*. Simon and Schuster.

Tart Ph.D., Charles. (2009). *The End of Materialism: How Evidence of the Paranormal Is Bringing Science and Spirit Together*. New Harbinger Publications.

Targ Ph.D., Russell. (2012). *The Reality of ESP: A Physicist's Proof of Psychic Abilities*. Quest Books.

Katz, Debra Lynne & Knowles, Jon. (2021). *Associative Remote Viewing: The Art & Science of Predicting Outcomes for Sports, Politics, Finances and the Lottery*. Living Dreams Press.

Warcollier, René. (2001). *Mind to Mind* (Studies in Consciousness). Hampton Roads Publishing.

McMoneagle, Joseph. (2000). *Remote Viewing Secrets: A Handbook*. Hampton Roads Publishing.

Smith Ph.D., Paul H. (2015). *The Essential Guide to Remote Viewing: The Secret Military Remote Perception Skill Anyone Can Learn*. Intentional Press.

## Recommended Reading

Swann, Ingo. (2018). *Everybody's Guide to Natural ESP: Unlocking the Extrasensory Power of Your Mind.* Swann-Ryder Productions, LLC.

Geller, Uri. (1975). *Uri Geller, My Story.* Praeger. *Also available to read online at https://www.urigeller.com/my-story/

Puharich, Andrija. (1974). *Uri: A journal of the mystery of Uri Geller.* Anchor Press. *Also available to read online at https://www.urigeller.com/uri-a-journal-of-the-mystery-of-uri-geller/

Strieber, Whitley & Kripal Ph.D., Jeffrey J. (2017). *The Super Natural: A New Vision of the Unexplained.* TarcherPerigee.

Dweck Ph.D., Carol S. (2007). *Mindset: The New Psychology of Success.* Ballantine Books.

Duckworth, Angela. (2018). *Grit: The Power of Passion and Perseverance.* Scribner.

Mischel Ph.D., Walter. (2015). *The Marshmallow Test: Why Self-Control Is the Engine of Success.* Little, Brown Spark.

Pink, Daniel H. (2011). *Drive: The Surprising Truth About What Motivates Us.* Riverhead Books.

# INDEX

| | | | |
|---|---|---|---|
| alpha brainwaves | 42 | telekinesis | 30, 37 |
| animals | 21 | teleportation | 3, 326 |
| anomalies | 38 | theta brainwaves | 32 |
| card (definition) | 38 | UFO | 9, 11 |
| CE-5 | 9 | windows of | |
| Chi Kung | 30, 37 | perception | 92 |
| children from China | 2, 3 | yoga | 30, 37 |
| crossing the midline | 48 | | |
| dermo-optical perception | 28, 31 | | |
| dream (stage) | 29, 40 | | |
| executive function | 38 | | |
| extra-terrestrial | 30 | | |
| guessing | 52 | | |
| hallucinations | 31 | | |
| hemispheric dominance | 46 | | |
| Hopkins, Lloyd F. | 5 | | |
| hypnosis | 28 | | |
| juggling | 48 | | |
| lottery | 34, 80 | | |
| meditation | 31, 32, 36, 44 | | |
| midbrain exercises | 48 | | |
| mindset | 33 | | |
| mitochondria | 37 | | |
| near-death experience | 29, 40 | | |
| neurons | 35 | | |
| out-of-body experience | 9, 29 | | |
| partner | 18, 20 | | |
| pilot study | 14 | | |
| psychic abilities | 22, 34, 36 | | |
| psychokinesis | 3, 326 | | |
| REM sleep | 29, 40 | | |
| Rhine, Joseph | 34 | | |
| Romains, Jules | 5 | | |
| seer (definition) | 32 | | |
| stress | 23, 36 | | |
| synapses | 32 | | |
| synesthesia | 32 | | |

# ABOUT THE AUTHOR

Sean McNamara lives in Denver, Colorado with his wife Cierra. He teaches meditation and consciousness exploration through his online courses, books, and in-person events.

The details of his life, including extraordinary psychic experiences not mentioned here, are described in his spiritual memoir, *Renegade Mystic: The Pursuit of Spiritual Freedom Through Consciousness Exploration*. It's available in various formats, including audiobook.

Learn more about him at www.MindPossible.com.

# Feel Inspired with Shirts and Hoodies from

## www.LearnMindSight.com

## and

## www.MindPossible.com

Made in the USA
Columbia, SC
05 April 2022

58535038R00187